D0209221

AN ANTHOLOGY OF
OLD ENGLISH POETRY

AN ANTHOLOGY OF

Old English Poetry

Translated into Alliterative Verse by

CHARLES W. KENNEDY

Murray Professor of English Literature, Emeritus
Princeton University

NEW YORK
OXFORD UNIVERSITY PRESS
1960

LIBRARY
COLLEGE OF SAN MATEO

PR
1508
K36

829
K38/a

© 1960 by Oxford University Press, Inc.

Library of Congress Catalogue Card Number: 59-11753

Printed in the United States of America

31524

SEP 30 '60

PREFACE

THIS Anthology is intended for readers who may wish to explore the riches of Old English poetry but find themselves shut out by the barrier of language. It has been my purpose to present in translation selections from Old English verse so chosen as to illustrate its variety of type, its scope of subject matter, and its poetic excellence. The task has been a pleasant one. We of the English tongue are fortunate heirs of a rich poetic heritage extending deep into European backgrounds, and written in England during the period from the seventh century to the end of the tenth.

From this body of poetry, it has been my endeavor to translate selections into a modern verse faithful to the Old English text and, as far as linguistic changes permit, suggestive of the alliterative rhythms of the Anglo-Saxon originals. In so sensitive a task success is not easy. The translator in the end can only hope that from this distant past these translations may catch some gleam of sunlight from an ancient world.

Of my translations in this volume some are old, some are new. My *Old English Elegies* and *The Earliest English Poetry* have for some time been out of print. I am happy to have this opportunity to republish the translations of the *Elegies*, as well as certain selections from *The Earliest English Poetry*. *The Battle of Maldon* I have newly translated and much of the poetry in the chapters dealing with the *Gnomic Verse* and the poems of Continental tradition. No Anthology could be adequate without illustration of the nature and quality of the longer poems such as *Beowulf*, the *Phoenix*, the Fall of Man from *Genesis*, and the Last Judgment of *Christ 3*. For permission to reprint selections from my translations of these poems in *Beowulf* and *Early English Christian Poetry*, I offer my sincere thanks to Oxford University Press.

Finally, for me there are interwoven with the lines of these poems long memories of pleasant association with graduate students at Princeton who were studying the language and literature of Anglo-Saxon England. They were both students and friends, and their friendship enriched the years.

C. W. K.

March 25, 1959
Princeton, N. J.

CONTENTS

INTRODUCTION *Page* ix

I ELEGIES AND DRAMATIC LYRICS: *The Wanderer; The Ruin; The Wife's Lament; The Husband's Message.* 1

II SEA POETRY: *The Seafarer; Noah's Flood; The Parting of the Red Sea; Helena Embarks for Palestine; St. Andrew's Voyage to Mermedonia; The Voyage of Life.* 15

III RIDDLES AND GNOMIC VERSE: *Anchor; Book-Moth; Cuckoo; Fish in River; Honey-Mead; Horn; Plow; Shield; Wild Swan; Wind;* Cotton MS *Maxims;* Exeter Book *Fates of Men;* Exeter Book *Maxims.* 37

IV CONTINENTAL TRADITION: *Deor's Lament; Widsith the Minstrel; The Tale of Sigemund; The Lay of Finn; The Battle of Finnsburg; Waldere; Charm for a Sudden Stitch; Charm for Unfruitful Land.* 53

V BEOWULF'S LAST BATTLE: *The Fire-Dragon and the Treasure; Beowulf and Wiglaf Slay the Dragon; Beowulf's Death; The Funeral Pyre.* 73

VI RELIGIOUS ALLEGORY: *The Whale; The Phoenix.* 95

VII OLD TESTAMENT AND APOCRYPHAL VERSE: *Lamentations of the Fallen Angels; The Temptation and Fall of Man.* 113

VIII CYNEWULF AND HIS FOLLOWERS: *Constantine's Vision of the Cross; Two Rune Signatures of Cynewulf; Advent Lyrics; A Dream of the Rood; The Last Judgment.* 131

IX HISTORIC BATTLE POEMS: *The Battle of Brunanburh; The Battle of Maldon.* 155

INDEX 171

INTRODUCTION

OLD ENGLISH POETRY, the Anglo-Saxon vernacular verse composed in England before the Norman Conquest, constitutes one of the richest medieval traditions in any modern European tongue. The period extending from the middle of the seventh century to the end of the tenth has left us a body of verse outstanding in variety and literary excellence. It was the product partly of an ancient culture which had come to England with the Germanic Settlement of the fifth and early sixth centuries, and partly of the transforming influences of the age in which it was written, an age of change and growth during which Germanic strains were slowly moulded by the influence of medieval learning and the Latin culture of the Christian Church.

The successive waves of the Settlement had brought to England a store of Continental tradition: myth and saga, folk-tale and chronicle, legends long known among the Germanic tribes, and now remembered and retold in England. A race does not easily lose memory of its past, even in the dark centuries and upon foreign soil. Tradition may grow obscure with passing years, and alien strains engraft themselves on ancient legend in strange and puzzling ways. But tradition persists, and the past lives on. In the songs of the early English, and in the lays that enlivened their banquets, old memories lingered, famous names and heroic deeds of chronicle and legend. The singer was an English minstrel, but often the song re-echoed a Continental past. Through the dusk of their great halls resounded the glory of heroes long dead: Attila the Hun and Eormanric the Goth, Theodoric and his thanes, Hildeburh of Finnsburg, Sigemund and Signy of the Volsungs, Walther of Aquitaine and his lady Hildegund, Beowulf of the Geats, shapes of the dead stirring to resurrection as the gleeman sang.

In this body of tradition came also the secret learning of the wise men and the folk-wisdom of the people: runic letters of mysterious meaning and power, magic charms against ill-fortune and disease, a folk-lore of herbs and simples, and the homely wisdoms of experience set forth in proverbs and gnomic verse. The Germanic Settlers carved their crude runic inscriptions on English stone, and on the utensils and weapons of early English life. In rude verse they chanted their pagan charms to defend their fields from barrenness, and their bodies from the aches and pains of rheumatic winters. In time of danger and doubt they appealed to the gnomic wisdom of their forefathers.

From of old the Settlers were at home on the sea, ranging widely in all weathers in their long, dragon-prowed Viking ships. As is true of all experienced mariners, their love of the salt sea-streams was tempered by a wholesome respect for the destructive might of ocean. *The Seafarer*, one of the most memorable of the elegies, celebrates at length, and with alternating stress, this bittersweet blending of attraction and fear. Old English poetry is filled with superb descriptive passages dealing with ocean-voyaging by night and day, in fair weather and foul.

The world of nature that hedged men about was stubborn and harsh.

The years were reckoned by the passing of the winters. Darkness and cold, the freezing hardships of winter on land and sea, the haunting fear of danger lurking in the shadows after the sun was gone, these are themes that set the grim mood for much of the early verse. But the long severity of their winter months brought by contrast a joy in returning Spring, "the sunny and shining days that ever observe their season," the time of "greening meadows and blossoming earth, and the music of bird-calls." Not a few passages of Old English verse contain brief, vivid realisms of Spring mood which make them memorable.

Much in the world of nature was of course unknown and terrifying. Superstitious imagination peopled the dark with warlocks and witches, gnomes and trolls, a malign and haunting crew of evil spirits. In their malevolent and capricious interference in the lives of men was to be found, it seemed, the secret source of misfortune such as sickness or loss of property, and of sudden tragic disaster for which no immediate cause seemed obvious. From this same mysterious nature were culled the means to combat such evils. Folk-knowledge of herbs and simples was blended with superstition in the fashioning of magic herbal decoctions used with rituals and formulas of transfer and exorcism. As time passed, these pagan charms were altered by the gradual influence of the Christian faith, and the sutures joining the ancient pagan and later Christian elements are often easily discernible. The *Charm for Unfruitful Land* is a case in point.

The Settlement brought with it simple codes of conduct and grim ways of life. Worship of the Germanic gods was a rude and savage cult. The ancient myths symbolized a titanic warfare between the kindlier forces of nature and those hostile powers by whose ruthless strength man's life and even the might of the gods themselves were menaced. Fate brooded over all, a dark inexorable power shrouded behind numbing hardship and mortal danger. To the living of life the strong man brought heroic courage and stoic endurance. Fate would sometimes spare, if valor held out.

The *Germania* of Tacitus provides a vivid estimate of the characteristics of early Germanic tribal life, out of which grew many of the qualities which entered into the Settlement of England. The stress on courage and the love of battle, reflected in so many passages of Old English verse, seem from the beginning to have been rooted in the Germanic strain. Personal loyalty and group loyalty were central in the moral code of the Settlers: loyalty to friend, to leader, and to clan. Loyalty to leader must be absolute. The spirit of the Germanic *comitatus*, with its reciprocal obligations of protection and reward on the one side, and loyalty and service on the other, colors the material of many a passage in Old English verse, and survives undiminished as late as *Maldon*. A retainer who had lost his lord was of all men most wretched, a lonely exile who could find no solace for his loss, no substitute for the tie that had been broken. The lament of *The Wanderer* is the classic passage for illustration of so tragic a grief.

The corpus of Old English verse gives evidence of the extent to which Englishmen of the seventh and eighth centuries still preserved race memories rooted in Germanic tradition, and enriched their poetry by borrowings from Continental legend and annals. Such poems as *Widsith*, *Deor's Lament*, and the *Waldere* and *Finnsburg* fragments, give testimony to this debt, as does the *Beowulf* in its tale of Sigemund, its lay of Finn, and its reflection of Scandinavian and Icelandic analogues.

With the conversion of England to the Christian faith there came a refinement of the scale of human values, a sensitizing of men's minds and moods, which swelled the currents of life, and varied and colored the play of poetic invention. To the early epic tales and songs of battle were added versifications of Biblical and Apocryphal themes, of lives of the saints, of martyrologies. The poetic mood turned from earlier forms to hymns of adoration, dream-visions, and prophetic verse. In this expansion, the reader is aware of the shaping energy of Christian learning: of the moulding force of Biblical exegesis and the Catholic liturgy, of Hexaemeral and Apocalyptic tradition, of ecclesiastical dogma and doctrine.

The religious poetry reflects both Classical and Christian culture. It is not to be forgotten that the poetry of the eighth and ninth centuries was written at a time when men of learning were familiar with the works of Aristotle and Cicero, or that Old English poetry contains elements that show the influence of Lucretius, Pliny, and Virgil. Alcuin's list of authors available in the Library at York includes their names, and Lucretius is cited and a line from the Sixth Book of Lucretius is quoted by Isidore of Seville, whose writings influenced the *De Natura Rerum* of Bede.

Most of all, these religious poems reveal their debt to the writings of medieval scholars: to Alcuin and Augustine, to Gregory and Bede, to Boethius and Lactantius, and to many others. In the fabric of this religious verse, moreover, threads of the earlier secular verse were blended.

Conventional elements of landscape and seascape, characteristic details of weather, a stereotyped imagery of loyalty and warfare, these are found as decorative elements in the religious poems.

Generally speaking, the authorship of this body of Old English verse, secular and religious, is almost unknown. Except for the Caedmon tradition as related by Bede, and the rune signatures of Cynewulf in *Juliana*, *Elene*, *Christ 2*, and the *Fates of the Apostles*, Old English poetry is of uncertain authorship and somewhat uncertain date. Caedmon's *Hymn* can be assigned to a date not far from 670. The spelling of Cynewulf's name in his runic signatures suggests the period from 750 to 800 for his signed poems. *Genesis B*, a dramatically vivid interpolation in the text of *Genesis*, is probably later than the middle of the ninth century, if its Old Saxon original is correctly dated as about 830 or 840. The battle poems of *Brunanburh* and *Maldon* were presumably written not long after the battles they commemorate, that is, 937, and 991.

Old English poetry was composed in a flexible type of four-stress, alliterative line consisting of two half-lines of two stresses each, separated by a strongly marked caesural pause. The stressed syllables established the rhythm, and the two half-lines were bound into a unit by the convention of alliteration. Variation in the relative positions of stresses within the line, and a convention of subordinate stresses, produced delicate and subtle currents of mutation and change of rhythm. The recitation of this alliterative verse was usually accompanied by chords struck on the harp.

The occurrence of rhyme is infrequent. Cynewulf uses it in a passage of fifteen lines near the end of the *Elene*, and a more extended passage is found in the eighty-seven lines of the *Rhyme Poem* of the Exeter Book. In a few other poems rhyme occurs in brief passages. Its occasional use may perhaps be traced to an influence of rhyming Latin hymns familiar to religious poets.

Estimated as a whole, Old English poetry expresses in many ways the changing spirit of the age. It was a period during which the limited perspectives of a pagan world were being gradually widened by the Christian philosophy. The stark and primitive social codes expressive of Germanic folkways were being transformed by the spiritual demands of Christian ethics. The Old English world was beginning to find room for a new frame of reference for the thoughts and strivings of men.

It will always remain true, I think, for many readers who love this ancient verse, that it stands as a testimonial, even if an imperfect one, of a way of life reborn and reshaped by the life-giving touch of the Christian faith, and the ecclesiastical culture of the medieval Church. As these influences enfranchised the thoughts and moulded the lives of men, their poetry, too, was transformed. The dark legends and narrow folkways of the pagan past died into silence, and poets sang with joy of a new way of life, and of the shining symbols which have served to shape the nature and destiny of the Christian world.

One of the dominant characteristics of the religious poetry is its fusion of sensitive religious faith with the shaping and vitalizing imagination and emotion of the poet. If the life of Cynewulf, for example, was in any way a cloistered one, his poetry is marked by no aloofness from the world. He was a lover of the human scene with a sense of its fugitive loveliness. He had a kindly understanding of the human heart.

In this body of Old English poetry much is excellent; a part is timeless. In it the old Germanic recognition of life's flinty necessities is still implicit, and strength-giving; as is also the conviction of man's imperative need of loyalty and courage. But the centuries of the English conversion had brought wider vision and longer thoughts. The heartbreak of the elegies, the fortitude of the battle poems, the antique grace and energy of the religious allegories, the gentle and lonely accents of Cynewulf, the lyric adoration of *A Dream of the Rood*, such poetry is memorable in any age. Finest of all is the *Beowulf*. In it, as in the poems of Cynewulf and his school, we find the most adequate poetic symbols of an age which touched life with the light of wider horizons, and shaped new hopes for the hearts of men.

I

ELEGIES AND DRAMATIC LYRICS

ELEGIES AND DRAMATIC LYRICS

The clear lyric strain which has poured its melody and passion into English verse through the centuries has early illustration in four Old English poems from the Exeter Book. Two of these lyrics, *The Wanderer* and *The Ruin*, are elegiac in mood. Two others, *The Wife's Lament* and *The Husband's Message*, are love poems or dramatic lyrics.

The two elegies differ markedly in mood and pattern from the personal elegy. Their range of interest is universal, deriving from a moving sense of the tragedy of life itself – a consciousness of the transience of earthly joy, and the inexorable limitation of man's existence by the mutable and mortal.

The Wanderer is the lament of a man who has lost his lord. Loosed from primitive loyalties to clan or leader, and lacking favor or protection, he has become in a very special sense a man adrift. Nowhere in Old English poetry has the misery attending this forlorn fate received more vivid, detailed, and emotional presentment.

The Ruin is an elegiac fragment setting forth the poet's musings on the ruins of a fortress, or city. Broken walls and towers, and shattered roofs of tile, now mark a site where once stood splendid banqueting halls and Roman baths. The reference to hot baths has led to a suggestion that the poem is describing Roman ruins of the city of Bath.

The Wife's Lament and *The Husband's Message* are in one sense companion poems, in another sense poems in contrast. The central theme of each poem is the separation of husband and wife. In *The Wife's Lament* her husband has crossed the sea, and in his absence his kinsmen, plotting a permanent separation of husband and wife, have condemned her to a dwelling in a solitary cave under an oak tree. Here she gives expression to her wretchedness and continuing love.

In *The Husband's Message* the husband has been forced by a vendetta to flee from his native land to a country beyond the sea. Now he sends back a "message staff" asking his wife to join him. The speaker is the staff itself telling how once it grew as a sapling near the sea. Now knife's point and man's skill have carved it with runic letters to bring a message only the wife can understand. The husband reminds her of the pledges they plighted of old. Now he has wealth and a lordly estate in a new land. One thing only he lacks – reunion with the "prince's daughter" to whom he is pledged. Let her take ship and sail to join him. At this point the five runic letters of the text assume at least a shadowy meaning. They may be the initial letters of five names, known to the wife, who stand as "oath-helpers," or guarantors of the husband's good faith, in this reaffirmation of his former vows.

The Wanderer

Oft to the Wanderer, weary of exile,
Cometh God's pity, compassionate love,
Though woefully toiling on wintry seas
With churning oar in the icy wave,
Homeless and helpless he fled from Fate.
Thus saith the Wanderer mindful of misery,
Grievous disasters, and death of kin:
"Oft when the day broke, oft at the dawning,
Lonely and wretched I wailed my woe.
No man is living, no comrade left,
To whom I dare fully unlock my heart.
I have learned truly the mark of a man
Is keeping his counsel and locking his lips,
Let him think what he will ! For, woe of heart
Withstandeth not Fate; a failing spirit
Earneth no help. Men eager for honor
Bury their sorrow deep in the breast.
"So have I also, often in wretchedness
Fettered my feelings, far from my kin,
Homeless and hapless, since days of old,
When the dark earth covered my dear lord's face,
And I sailed away with sorrowful heart,
Over wintry seas, seeking a gold-lord,
If far or near lived one to befriend me
With gift in the mead-hall and comfort for grief.
"Who bears it, knows what a bitter companion,
Shoulder to shoulder, sorrow can be,
When friends are no more. His fortune is exile,
Not gifts of fine gold; a heart that is frozen,
Earth's winsomeness dead. And he dreams of the hall-men,
The dealing of treasure, the days of his youth,
When his lord bade welcome to wassail and feast.

But gone is that gladness, and never again
Shall come the loved counsel of comrade and king.
"Even in slumber his sorrow assaileth,
And, dreaming he claspeth his dear lord again,
Head on knee, hand on knee, loyally laying,
Pledging his liege as in days long past.
Then from his slumber he starts lonely-hearted,
Beholding gray stretches of tossing sea,
Sea-birds bathing, with wings outspread,
While hailstorms darken, and driving snow.
Bitterer then is the bane of his wretchedness,
The longing for loved one: his grief is renewed.
The forms of his kinsmen take shape in the silence;
In rapture he greets them; in gladness he scans
Old comrades remembered. But they melt into air
With no word of greeting to gladden his heart.
Then again surges his sorrow upon him;
And grimly he spurs his weary soul
Once more to the toil of the tossing sea.
"No wonder therefore, in all the world,
If a shadow darkens upon my spirit
When I reflect on the fates of men—
How one by one proud warriors vanish
From the halls that knew them, and day by day
All this earth ages and droops unto death.
No man may know wisdom till many a winter
Has been his portion. A wise man is patient,
Not swift to anger, nor hasty of speech,
Neither too weak, nor too reckless, in war,
Neither fearful nor fain, nor too wishful of wealth,
Nor too eager in vow— ere he know the event.
A brave man must bide when he speaketh his boast
Until he know surely the goal of his spirit.
"A wise man will ponder how dread is that doom
When all this world's wealth shall be scattered and waste

As now, over all, through the regions of earth,
Walls stand rime-covered and swept by the winds.
The battlements crumble, the wine-halls decay;
Joyless and silent the heroes are sleeping
Where the proud host fell by the wall they defended.
Some battle launched on their long, last journey;
One a bird bore o'er the billowing sea;
One the gray wolf slew; one a grieving eorl
Sadly gave to the grave's embrace.
The Warden of men hath wasted this world
Till the sound of music and revel is stilled,
And these giant-built structures stand empty of life.
"He who shall muse on these mouldering ruins,
And deeply ponder this darkling life,
Must brood on old legends of battle and bloodshed,
And heavy the mood that troubles his heart:
'Where now is the warrior? Where is the war horse?
Bestowal of treasure, and sharing of feast?
Alas! the bright ale-cup, the byrny-clad warrior,
The prince in his splendor —those days are long sped
In the night of the past, as if they never had been!'
And now remains only, for warriors' memorial,
A wall wondrous high with serpent shapes carved.
Storms of ash-spears have smitten the eorls,
Carnage of weapon, and conquering Fate.
"Storms now batter these ramparts of stone;
Blowing snow and the blast of winter
Enfold the earth; night-shadows fall
Darkly lowering, from the north driving
Raging hail in wrath upon men.
Wretchedness fills the realm of earth,
And Fate's decrees transform the world.
Here wealth is fleeting, friends are fleeting,
Man is fleeting, maid is fleeting;
All the foundation of earth shall fail!"

Thus spake the sage in solitude pondering.
Good man is he who guardeth his faith.
He must never too quickly unburden his breast
Of its sorrow, but eagerly strive for redress;
And happy the man who seeketh for mercy
From his heavenly Father, our Fortress and Strength.

The Ruin

Wondrous this masonry wasted by Fate!
Giant-built battlements shattered and broken!
The roofs are in ruin, the towers are wrecked,
The frost-covered bastions battered and fallen.
Rime whitens mortar; the cracking walls
Have sagged and toppled, weakened by Time.
The clasp of earth and the clutch of the grave
Grip the proud builders, long perished and gone,
While a hundred generations have run.
Hoary with lichen and ruddy of hue
This wall has outlasted, unshaken by storm,
Reign after reign; now ravaged and wrecked
The lofty arch is leveled in ruin. . . .
Firmly the builder laid the foundations,
Cunningly bound them with iron bands;
Stately the palaces, splendid the baths,
Towers and pinnacles pointing on high;
Many a mead-hall rang with their revelry,
Many a court with the clangor of arms,
Till Fate the all-leveling laid them low.
A pestilence rose and corpses were rife,
And death laid hold on the warrior-host.
Then their bulwarks were broken, their fortresses fell,
The hands to restore them were helpless and still.
Desolate now are the courts, and the dome,

With arches discolored, is stripped of its tiles.
Where of old once the warrior walked in his pride,
Gleaming with gold and wanton with wine,
Splendidly shining in glittering mail,
The structure lies fallen and scattered in ruin.
Around him he saw a treasure of silver,
Riches of pearl and precious stones,
In a shining city of far-flung sway.
There stood courts of stone, with a gushing spring
Of boiling water in welling floods,
And a wall embosomed in gleaming embrace
The spot where the hot baths burst into air.

The Wife's Lament

A song I sing of sorrow unceasing,
The tale of my trouble, the weight of my woe,
Woe of the present, and woe of the past,
Woe never-ending of exile and grief,
But never since girlhood greater than now.
First, the pang when my lord departed,
Far from his people, beyond the sea;
Bitter the heartache at break of dawn,
The longing for rumor in what far land
So weary a time my loved one tarried.
Far I wandered then, friendless and homeless,
Seeking for help in my heavy need.
  With secret plotting his kinsmen purposed
To wedge us apart, wide worlds between,
And bitter hate. I was sick at heart.
Harshly my lord bade lodge me here.
In all this land I had few to love me,
Few that were loyal, few that were friends.
Wherefore my spirit is heavy with sorrow
To learn my beloved, my dear man and mate
Bowed by ill-fortune and bitter in heart,
Is masking his purpose and planning a wrong.
With blithe hearts often of old we boasted
That nought should part us save death alone;
All that has failed and our former love
Is now as if it had never been!
Far or near where I fly there follows
The hate of him who was once so dear.
  In this forest-grove they have fixed my abode
Under an oak in a cavern of earth,
An old cave-dwelling of ancient days,
Where my heart is crushed by the weight of my woe.
Gloomy its depths and the cliffs that o'erhang it,
Grim are its confines with thorns overgrown—

A joyless dwelling where daily the longing
For an absent loved one brings anguish of heart.
  Lovers there are who may live their love,
Joyously keeping the couch of bliss,
While I in my earth-cave under the oak
Pace to and fro in the lonely dawn.
Here must I sit through the summer-long day,
Here must I weep in affliction and woe;
Yet never, indeed, shall my heart know rest
From all its anguish, and all its ache,
Wherewith life's burdens have brought me low.
  Ever man's years are subject to sorrow,
His heart's thoughts bitter, though his bearing be blithe;
Troubled his spirit, beset with distress—
Whether all wealth of the world be his lot,
Or hunted by Fate in a far country
My beloved is sitting soul-weary and sad,
Swept by the storm, and stiff with the frost,
In a wretched cell under rocky cliffs
By severing waters encircled about—
Sharpest of sorrows my lover must suffer
Remembering always a happier home.
Woeful his fate whose doom is to wait
With longing heart for an absent love.

The Husband's Message

In the sand I grew, by the rocky sea-wall
Near the surf firm-rooted in fixed abode.
Few were the men who beheld my refuge
In the lonely reaches beside the sea;
Only the dark wave at the day's dawning
Sportively bound me in flowing embrace.
Little I weened that I, who was voiceless,
Should ever hold speech, or discourse at the feast.
That is a marvel amazing the mind
Of those who know little of such-like things
How a knife's sharp edge, and a strong hand's skill,
Steel's keen point, and man's cunning craft,
Purposely planned me, assigned me my part
To give thee a message that we two may grasp,
To utter it boldly, yet so that no other
May publish abroad the words I report.
To thine ear only I tell the tale
How first as a sapling I flourished and grew. . . .
In the hold of a ship, o'er the salt sea-streams,
Where my liege lord sent me oft I have sailed.
Now in a bark's bosom here am I borne.
Now shalt thou learn of my lord's loyal love;
His enduring affection I dare to affirm.
Lady ring-laden, he bade me implore thee,
Who carved this wood, that thou call to mind
The pledges you plighted before you were parted,
While still in the same land together you shared
A lordly home and the rapture of love,
Before a feud drove him far from his folk.
He it is bids me eagerly urge
When from the hill slope, out of the wood,
Thou hearest the cuckoo plaintively calling,
Haste thee to ship on the tossing sea.
Let no living man, then, delay thee in sailing,

Stay thee in leaving or stop thee in flight.
  Spread thy sail on the home of the sea-mew,
Take seat in thy galley, and steer away south
To where o'er the sea-lane thy lover awaits.
No greater bliss could his heart engage
In all the world —'twas his word to me—
If God the Almighty would grant you two
To dwell together and deal out gifts,
To tried retainers, of treasure and rings.
He hath abundance of beaten gold. . . .
Now in a far land my lord holds in fee
Home and fair fields though here once of old,
Fated and lonely, need forced him to flight,
Launching his ship on the lanes of the deep,
Churning the sea-streams in haste to escape.
  Now his troubles are over and all distress,
He lacks no wealth that the heart may wish,
Jewels and horses and joys of the hall,
Nor any fair treasure that earth can afford.
O Prince's daughter! if he may possess thee,
To add to the pledges ye plighted of old,
Here S and R together I set,
EA, W, and D, by oath to declare
That while life lasts so long he'll be faithful
To lover's vow and to true love's pledge
Which often ye plighted in days of old.

II

SEA POETRY

SEA POETRY

English poetry from the beginning has had as a favorite theme the influence in men's lives of the varying moods and might of the sea. From the Old English period it has reflected the actualities of ocean life with such faithful directness that the poetic rendering is as expressive of the nineteenth century as of the ninth.

This strain in Old English verse is well illustrated by portions of six poems which include the theme of ocean-voyaging: *The Seafarer* of the Exeter Book; *Noah's Flood* from *Genesis*; *The Parting of the Red Sea* from *Exodus*; *Helena Embarks for Palestine* from Cynewulf's *Elene*; *The Voyage of Life* from Cynewulf's *Christ 2*; and *St. Andrew's Voyage to Mermedonia* from *Andreas*.

In *The Seafarer* the hardship, loneliness, and danger of wintry voyages in uncharted seas, and the lure and fascination that intertwine even with knowledge of peril, these attributes of the sailor's life are set forth with sensitive faithfulness. *Noah's Flood* follows the simplicity of Biblical narrative. But there is poetic vividness in the description of the rains that caused the Flood, and a touch of Old English realism in the birds that Noah sends out from the ark. The raven is depicted as the Old English battle-scavenger. The foul one "perched on the floating corpses. The dusky-feathered would not return." The dove, in its three flights to scan the receding waters, is drawn with warm touches that suggest the intimacy of St. Guthlac and the birds. Similarly, in *The Parting of the Red Sea* a naïvely realistic visualization of uncovered ocean-bottoms, whereon man's foot had never been set before, makes the passage memorable.

Helena Embarks for Palestine, brief as it is, is one of the most finished of these sea-voyages, combining a detailed embarkation scene with the voyage itself, and ending with the debarkation and march inland. *The Voyage of Life* is an illustration of Cynewulf's poetic skill in expanding Gregory's brief suggestion about "fixing the anchor of hope upon an eternal fatherland" into an artistically complete and detailed ocean simile.

The most sustained account of an ocean voyage in Old English poetry is the voyage of St. Andrew to Mermedonia. Andrew's voyage, undertaken at God's command, is in a ship of which God Himself is Shipman and two angels the sailors, although throughout the voyage they remain unknown. With these elements of miracle are combined some of the finest realisms in Old English sea poetry. The sailing at daybreak (235-351), the storm at sea (369-381), and Andrew's expression of his admiration of the Shipman's seamanship (471-520), are superbly done.

The Seafarer *

A song I sing of my sea-adventure,
The strain of peril, the stress of toil,
Which oft I endured in anguish of spirit
Through weary hours of aching woe.
My bark was swept by the breaking seas;
Bitter the watch from the bow by night
As my ship drove on within sound of the rocks.
My feet were numb with the nipping cold,
Hunger sapped a sea-weary spirit,
And care weighed heavy upon my heart.
  Little the landlubber, safe on shore,
Knows what I've suffered in icy seas
Wretched and worn by the winter storms,
Hung with icicles, stung by hail,
Lonely and friendless and far from home.
In my ears no sound but the roar of the sea,
The icy combers, the cry of the swan;
In place of the mead-hall and laughter of men
My only singing the sea-mew's call,
The scream of the gannet, the shriek of the gull;
Through the wail of the wild gale beating the bluffs
The piercing cry of the ice-coated petrel,
The storm-drenched eagle's echoing scream.
In all my wretchedness, weary and lone,
I had no comfort of comrade or kin.
  Little indeed can he credit, whose town-life
Pleasantly passes in feasting and joy,
Sheltered from peril, what weary pain
Often I've suffered in foreign seas.
Night shades darkened with driving snow
From the freezing north, and the bonds of frost
Firm-locked the land, while falling hail,

* *The Seafarer* 1–64.

Coldest of kernels, encrusted earth.
  Yet still, even now, my spirit within me
Drives me seaward to sail the deep,
To ride the long swell of the salt sea-wave.
Never a day but my heart's desire
Would launch me forth on the long sea-path,
Fain of far harbors and foreign shores.
Yet lives no man so lordly of mood,
So eager in giving, so ardent in youth,
So bold in his deeds, or so dear to his lord,
Who is free from dread in his far sea-travel,
Or fear of God's purpose and plan for his fate.
The beat of the harp, and bestowal of treasure,
The love of woman, and worldly hope,
Nor other interest can hold his heart
Save only the sweep of the surging billows;
His heart is haunted by love of the sea.
  Trees are budding and towns are fair,
Meadows kindle and all life quickens,
All things hasten the eager-hearted,
Who joyeth therein, to journey afar,
Turning seaward to distant shores.
The cuckoo stirs him with plaintive call,
The herald of summer, with mournful song,
Foretelling the sorrow that stabs the heart.
Who liveth in luxury, little he knows
What woe men endure in exile's doom.
  Yet still, even now, my desire outreaches,
My spirit soars over tracts of sea,
O'er the home of the whale, and the world's expanse.
Eager, desirous, the lone sprite returneth;
It cries in my ears and it urges my heart
To the path of the whale and the plunging sea.

Noah's Flood *

Then the Lord God spoke and said unto Noah:
"With a great flood I will destroy this folk
And every kind of living creature
That fill the sky and swim the sea,
Birds of air, and beasts of the field.
But thou shalt be saved, and thy sons also,
When the dark waters, the destroying deep,
Shall swallow the hosts of sinful men.
  "Begin to build thee a ship, a mighty wave-house;
Make room for many and a rightful place
For every creature, each after its kind.
Build floors in the ark's bosom;
Fashion it well fifty ells wide,
Thirty ells high, three hundred ells long,
And fasten it firm against the flood.
Within it lead offspring of all that live,
Seed of all flesh, and the ark shall hold them."...
  After many winters All-Wielding God
Saw the greatest of sea-houses towering high,
Noah's vessel well fastened within and without,
And preserved with pitch against the flood.
It was best of all ships, a special kind
Growing more safe as the breaking seas
And black sea-streams beat up against it....
  And Noah embarked boarding the wave-ship
As God gave bidding, leading his sons
And their wives with them; and all God willed
To preserve for seed went into the ark
As the Almighty had given command.
There behind them the Warden of heaven,
The Lord of victory, locked the door
Of the ocean-house with His own hands,

* *Genesis* 1294–1313; 1320–26; 1356–99; 1441–82.

And with His blessing the Lord God blessed
All in the ark. Now the son of Lamech,
Old and wise, had six hundred winters
When he boarded the ark with dear ones and sons.
Then the Lord unloosed the rain from the heavens,
Let roaring torrents and rushing streams
From every channel overflow the world.
Over the shore's barrier the sea surged up;
Strong was He and stern Who ruled the waters!
The dark flood covered the children of evil,
Laid waste their realm and their native land.
God visited their sins on the sons of men!
For forty days and forty nights
The sea laid hold on that fated folk.
Fierce the affliction and deadly to men;
The stormy surges of the King of glory
Snatched life from body of those sinful men.
The raging flood, heaving beneath the heavens
Covered high hills throughout the wide world,
On its bosom uplifted the ark from the earth
And all living things which the Lord had blessed
When He locked behind them the door of the ship.
Then over the deep, under the heavens,
That best of dwellings and the burden it bore
Were driven afar. No watery terror
Could touch those sailors for Holy God
Saved them and ferried them. Fifteen ells deep
Over the hills lay the heaving flood.
'Twas a fearful fate! . . .
Then after long days the son of Lamech
From the ark let fly a black-feathered raven
Over the steep flood. Noah counted it sure,
If in its flight it could find no land,
The raven would return unto the ark
Over the wide waters. But Noah's hope failed!
The foul one perched on the floating corpses;
The dusky-feathered would not return.

Then seven days after the dark raven,
He let a gray dove over the deep
Fly from the ark to try if the flood
Had ebbed from the ground of the green earth.
Widely she sought her desire circling afar
But nowhere found rest. Because of the flood
She could find no land with her feet,
Nor light on a leaf of any tree
Because of the sea-streams. The steep hills
Were covered with water. The wild bird
Flew back at evening over the dusky waves
Unto the ark settling weary,
And hungry, into the hand of that holy man.
And again after seven days a second wild dove
Was sent from the ark. She flew afar,
Exulting in flight, till she found a perch
And resting place in a tree. She was happy-hearted
That weary of wing she could sit on the shining boughs.
She shook her feathers and flew back with her gift,
To Noah's hand bringing a twig of an olive tree,
With leaves growing green. The lord of the shipmen knew
That comfort at last was come, requital for danger and toil.
And after a third week Noah sent out a dove;
But she flew not back to the ark. She found dry land,
And came to green forests. Never again
Would she rest glad-hearted under the ark's dark roof.
Nor was there need!

The Parting of the Red Sea *

The band of the bold were gathered together,
Ready to advance; their banner rode high,
Brightest of beacons. And all abode
Nigh to the sea till their gleaming guide
Broke the cloud barrier, shining on shield.
  Then before the host a herald stood forth,
A valiant leader uplifting his shield,
Commanding the captains to silence their troops
That many might hear their lord's behest.
The people's shepherd fain would speak
With holy voice before the host;
In words of worth their leader addressed them:
"Fear not though Pharaoh may bring against us
An army of sword-men, a legion of eorls.
This day our God shall give them reward!
They shall not live longer to vex us with woe;
Have no fear of the doomed, or the fated for death.
Their fleeting race has run to its end. . . .
  "Watch, dear people; behold a wonder:
With right hand grasping this green rod
I smote the sea. The waves rise up,
The waters form a rampart wall.
The sea is thrust aside! The sands are dry,
Gray army-roads, ancient foundations
(Whereon I never in all the world
Heard said that man set foot before),
Shining plains, imprisoned deep-sea bottoms
Which from of old the waters covered with waves.
The South Wind, breath of the ocean,
Has blown them back. The deep is divided.
The ebb tide spewed up sand. And well I know
God, the Almighty, has granted you grace,

* *Exodus* 247–68; 278–306.

You bronze-clad eorls! Now haste is best
That you may be free from clutch of the foe,
Since God has raised these Red Sea streams
Into a rampart. The walls of water are reared
To the roof of clouds, a wondrous road in the sea."
After these words the warriors rose,
The band of the valiant. The sea lay still.
On the sand the legion uplifted their banners,
Their bright linden bucklers. For Israel's host
The wall of water stood upright all the long day;
The resolute eorls were shielded with sure defense.

Helena Embarks for Palestine *

Then Constantine, mindful of the Holy Cross,
Bade his mother fare over the floodway
To search with many where the Tree of splendor,
The Holy Rood, was hid in earth,
The Cross of heaven's King. Nor was Helena slow
In sailing, nor slighted the word of her son,
Her giver of good. Soon was she ready
For the pleasing voyage as the prince of men,
Of mail-clad warriors, gave her command.
A host of eorls made haste to the shore;
Sea-horses stood ready at the ocean's rim,
Bridled sea-stallions breasting the waves.
The lady's departure was plain to see
As she moved with her train to the tumbling breakers.
Many a stately man stood on the shore
Of the Wendel-Sea. Swiftly they hurried
Over the border-paths, band after band.
They loaded the vessels with byrny and lance,
With men in bucklers, with battle-sarks,
With man and maid. O'er the sea-monsters' home
They drove their foaming deep-flanked ships.
Oft on the waves the stout wood stood
The blows of the billows. The ocean roared.
Never learned I early or late
Of lady who led on the ocean-lanes
Fairer band o'er the paths of the flood.
There might he see who beheld that sailing
Sea-wood scud under swelling sails,
Sea-steeds plunge and break through the billows,
Wave-ships skim. The warriors bold
Were blithe, and the queen had joy of the journey.
When the high-prowed ships had come to their haven

* Cynewulf's *Elene* 212–65.

Over the ocean in the Grecian land
They left their vessels much tossed of the tides,
Their old sea-homes, at the ocean's shore
Fast at anchor to await on the waves
The fate of the band, when the battle-queen
With her troop of warriors o'er the eastern ways
Should seek them again. Then was easily seen
Woven mail on many an eorl
Choicest of blades, bright battle-byrny,
Visored casque and fair boar-crest;
There men of war were on the march,
A convoy of warriors around their queen.
The stalwart heroes, heralds of Caesar,
Gaily fared through the Grecian land,
Men of battle in shining mail;
And many a gem in its jeweled setting
Gleamed in that war-host, the gift of a lord.

St. Andrew's Voyage to Mermedonia *

A Voice from heaven was heard on earth
In the land of Achaia where Andrew lodged
Leading the people in the way of Life.
To the great-hearted hero the Glory of kings,
Lord of hosts and Maker of men,
Opened His mind-hoard, uttered this word:
  "Go forth straightway faring afar
To seek the coasts where the Cannibals dwell
With murderous fury defending their land.
Such is their custom that in that country
No foreign man is allowed to live;
If it be that they find one defenseless there
Deadly torture and death is his lot.
In bondage of chains your brother lies
Among that people. Three nights from now
Through heathen hatred, smitten with spears,
He shall send forth his soul on a far journey
Except ere that hour you haste to help."
  Unto Him promptly Andrew replied:
"O God of heaven and Lord of glory,
How can I fare on so far a course
Over the deep ocean so soon as Thou sayest?
But this Thine angel may easily do.
From heaven he sees the ocean-stretches,
All the swan-road and the salt sea-streams,
The tumult of waves, the water-terror,
The ways that lengthen across wide lands.
I have no friends in that foreign folk,
I know not the mind of any man there,
And the ocean-ways across the cold water
To me are unknown."
  Then God made answer:

* *Andreas* 167–224; 235–76; 290–326; 343–51; 359–414; 465–536.

"Alas! Andrew! that ever your heart
Should be slow to this journey! Slight were the task
For God Almighty to command on earth,
Under the sun, that the city be moved
Unto this country, the stately seat
And all who live there, if the Lord of glory
Decreed it by His word. You may not weary
In this wayfaring, nor waver in heart
If you think to keep covenant, compact with God.
"At the hour be ready. In performing this errand
Can be no delay. You shall risk your life;
The path shall lead to the power of the foe
Where the crash of battle shall come upon you,
The war-might of heroes and heathen strife.
In the early dawn with the coming of day
At the ocean's margin straightway take ship
And drive through the surges on the cold sea.
My blessing go with you where you go.". . .
Then Andrew at dawn at the break of day
Over the sand dunes strode to the shore
Keen of courage, his comrades beside him
Tramping the shingle. The ocean resounded,
The combers crashed. The hero rejoiced
When he saw at the sea's edge a broad-beamed boat.
Morning sun came, the brightest of beacons,
Heaven's candle flaming over the flood,
Holy light dawning out of the dark.
He saw there waiting three stately sailors
Geared for the voyage, great-hearted men
In their wave-boat sitting as if come from over sea.
'Twas the Lord Himself, the Leader of men,
Almighty, Eternal, with His angels twain.
They were garbed like mariners, seafaring men,
When they plunge in their keels over cold water
On a far journey o'er the flood's expanse.
Ready for sea as he stood on the shingle
Andrew bespoke them with hearty hail:

"Sea-crafty men, whence come you sailing
In your ocean-plunger, your peerless bark?
Whence have the sea-streams brought your ship
O'er the tossing main?"
The Almighty made answer
As if He wist not what man it was
Of mortal men who awaited His word,
With whom He held speech on the sandy shore:
"From the Mermedonian folk we have come faring
On a far journey. Over the flood
Dowered with speed our swift sea-stallion,
Our high-prowed courser, carried us on
Along the whale-path until at last
We came to this country urged by the waves
As the wind drove us."
Humble of heart
Andrew made answer: "A boon I would beg
Though I've little to give of treasure or gold,
That you take us along in your tall-sided ship,
Your high-prowed floater, o'er the home of the whale
To the place of that people. And God will reward
Your kindness to us in this ocean-crossing.". . .
The Prince of angels made reply,
The Saviour of men, from the ship's prow:
"Gladly will we bear you o'er the fishes' bath
To the land that your longing leads you to seek
When you have paid toll, the appointed tribute,
Even as sailors over the ship's side
Are willing to agree."
Then Andrew gave answer
Friendless, penniless, making reply:
"I have no gold, no goodly treasure,
No food or riches or woven rings,
No land or linked jewels, to spur your desire
Or whet your willingness as your words suggest."
The Sovereign of men where He sat on the gangway
Said unto Andrew o'er the breaking seas:

"How does it happen, dearest friend,
That lacking money you would make a voyage
O'er the climbing billows, past the cold cliffs,
To the far sea-limits? Have you no food
To bring you comfort, or clear water
For your refreshment, on the ocean-flood?
Hard is the life for one who long
Tries ocean-voyaging."
Andrew in answer,
Wise of wit, his word-hoard unlocked:
"Ill befits it since God has given you
Food and fortune and worldly wealth
That you question me thus with cruel pride
And bitter word. Better a man
Hail the wayfarer with humble heart
And kindly spirit, as Christ once bade,
Our glorious Warden. We are His thanes,
His chosen champions. He is True King,
God and Ruler of celestial glory,
One Lord Eternal of every created thing," . . .
Eternal God answered:
"If, as you say, you are His servants
Who raised up heaven high above earth,
And have kept the law of the Holy Lord,
Gladly will I sail you over the sea-flood
As you have begged." Then the heroes brave,
Bold of spirit, embarked in the ship
And their hearts rejoiced in the ocean-journey. . . .
There the saint took seat near to the Shipman,
Noble beside noble. Never did I hear
Of fairer vessel more richly freighted
With stately treasure. Within it sat
Glorious princes, and goodly thanes.
And the Powerful Prince, Eternal and Mighty,
Bade His angel, His honored thane,
Bring food to nourish those needy men
On the thronging billows, that they might the better

Endure their lot on the surging deep.
Then the depths were troubled. The horn-fish darte
Gliding through ocean; the gray gull wheeled
Searching for carrion. The sun grew dark,
A gale arose and great waves broke;
The sea-streams were stirred. Halyards were humming,
Sails were drenched. Sea-terror grew
In the welter of waves. The thanes were adread
Who sailed with Andrew on the ocean-stream,
Nor hoped with life ever to come to land.
Not yet was it known Who steered their ship
Through the breaking seas.
Then again the saint
As a loyal thane thanked his Great Leader
On the ocean-highway, the oar-stirred sea,
Because his strength had been stayed with food.
"For this repast may the Righteous Ruler
Author of life, and Lord of hosts,
Grant you reward, and give you for food
The bread of heaven because you accorded me
Love and good will on the mountainous waves.
My youthful warriors, willing thanes,
Are sorely troubled. The sea resounds,
The surging ocean; the depths are stirred,
Terribly shaken. My troop are aghast,
My force of brave followers deeply dismayed."
Then from the helm spoke the Maker of men:
"Let us steer the ship, our floater, to shore
O'er the ocean-main and there let your men
Tarry on land until you return."
But straightway the eorls, strong to endure,
Gave Him answer; they would not agree
That they should forsake at the vessel's stem
Their beloved leader and choose the land:
"If we desert you whither shall we wander
Lordless and lonely, lacking all good?
We shall be loathed in every land,

Hated of all men where valiant heroes
Sit in assembly holding debate
Who best has bolstered his lord in battle
When hand and buckler were bearing the brunt,
Hacked with swords, on the field of fate." . . .
Then the waves subsided, the sea's fierce tumult;
The rush of the waters was turned away.
The saint's heart was happy that the terror was past.
Sage of counsel he began to speak,
Wise of wit he unlocked his word-hoard:
  "Never have I met more skillful mariner
Or more sea-crafty than you seem to me;
No stouter sailor, none sager in counsel
Or wiser in word. A boon I would beg
Illustrious eorl, though it's little I have
Of goodly treasure or gifts of gold.
Gladly would I gain, O glorious Prince,
Your welcome friendship if I may win it,
And you shall have grace and holy hope
In heavenly glory if you'll graciously share
Your wise counsels with sea-weary men.
O noble hero, since the Maker of men,
Our King, has granted you glory and might,
One art from you I am eager to learn:
If you will teach me how you sail your ship,
Your spray-drenched floater, across the sea.
  "Sixteen voyages early and late
It has been my lot to sail in my sea-boat
With freezing hands as I smote the sea,
The ocean-stream. This now is another.
Never have I known one like to you
Of the sons of men steering over stem.
The roaring billows beat on the strand;
Full swift is this bark and most like a bird
Foamy-necked faring over the waves.
Full well I know I never have seen
In any sailor more wondrous sea-craft.

Most like it is as if on land
The boat stood still where wind and storm
Could stir it not, nor breaking billows
Shatter the high prow; yet it speeds over ocean
Swift under sail. You yourself are young,
O warden of warriors, man of the sea;
Not many your winters! Yet in your mind
You have an eorl's answers; in any assembly
You have wise understanding of every word."
  God the Eternal made answer to Andrew:
"Oft it befalls on the watery way
That storms arise as we break through the billows
In ships with sailors, in our ocean-steeds.
At times it goes hard with us on the high seas
Even though we survive the perilous voyage.
But never may Ocean work ill to any
Against God's will. He governs life
Who binds the seas, Who bridles and fetters
The dark flood. Over every folk
He rules by right Who raised up the heavens,
With His hands fastened and fixed their support.
That bright habitation He filled with bliss,
By His sole might blessed the abode of angels.
  "Now is it known and clearly disclosed
That you are His servant Who sits in glory,
For the sea perceived, the circle of ocean,
That you had the gift of the Holy Ghost.
The billows abated, the tumult of breakers;
The terror was stilled and the wide-stretching waves.
The seas subsided when the water saw
That He Whose might shaped heavenly glory
In His safe-keeping held you close."

The Voyage of Life *

Now is it most like as if on ocean
Across cold water we sail in our keels,
Over the wide sea in our ocean-steeds,
Faring on in our flood-wood. Fearful the stream,
The tumult of waters, whereon we toss
In this feeble world. Fierce are the surges
On the ocean-lanes. Hard was our life
Before we made harbor over the foaming seas.
Then help was vouchsafed when God's Spirit-Son
Guided us to the harbor of salvation and granted us grace
That we may understand over the ship's side
Where to moor our sea-steeds, our ocean-stallions,
Fast at anchor. Let us fix our hope
Upon that haven which the Lord of heaven,
In holiness on high, has opened by His Ascension.

* *Christ* 2 850–66.

III

RIDDLES AND GNOMIC VERSE

RIDDLES AND GNOMIC VERSE

Included in the Exeter Book and the Cotton MS are excellent examples of two highly conventionalized types of Old English verse: the gatherings of versified riddles, and of versified maxims, or gnomes.

The Old English *Riddles* compose a series of thumbnail sketches of the daily realisms of Old English life. They are in a certain sense a listing of the things with which man's life was woven: the birds and animals of country life, man's food and drink, the tools with which he worked, the armor and weapons with which he fought, his instruments of music. By their range and detailed vividness the *Riddles* supplement the pictures of Old English culture derived from the narrative poems.

It is clear, moreover, that in the shaping of these vernacular *Riddles* there was Latin influence. This was in part exerted by various collections of Latin riddles current among scholars in the eighth century, among others the riddles of Symphosius and Ealdhelm. However, quite aside from any influence of these Latin riddles, there is in the Old English *Riddles* 1, and 2-3, unmistakable evidence of the poet's familiarity with theories of meteorology set forth by Lucretius in the sixth book of the *De Natura*, and by Pliny in the second book of the *Natural History*. It is this Classical theory of meteorology that underlies the sustained imagery of the Old English "Storm" *Riddles*.

The gnomic strain runs like a clearly visible thread through the entire body of Old English poetry. It is found in concentrated form in the *Gnomic Verses*, or *Maxims*, of the Exeter Book and the Cotton MS. But, in addition, many passages in Old English lyric and narrative verse reveal the gnomic mood. The gnome was employed as a brief, pithy, sententious saying, sometimes to set forth proverbial or folk wisdom, sometimes to express generations of keen-eyed observation of nature, sometimes to give folk sanction to a moral, or to define a virtue or vice. A knowledge of the more characteristic gnomes was evidently a part of the literary endowment of an Old English poet.

In lines 94-106 of the Exeter Book *Maxims* we find a passage that may possibly be an insertion into a broken text. These lines, coming abruptly as they do, are in themselves notable for preserving a charming vignette of Old English domestic life, a sailor's home-coming. The wife welcomes home her bread-winner, washes his garments stained by the sea, gives him fresh raiment, responds to his love. The fact that the poet specifically refers to the wife as a Frisian, coming as it does without explanation, falls somewhat strangely on the ear. But the Frisians in England came of seafaring stock, and there were Frisians among the sailors who manned King Alfred's navy. There is also evidence suggesting that in the eighth century a Frisian community existed at York.

Riddles *

Anchor

Oft I must strive with wind and wave,
Battle them both when under the sea
I feel out the bottom, a foreign land.
In lying still I am strong in the strife;
If I fail in that they are stronger than I
And, wrenching me loose, soon put me to rout.
They wish to capture what I must keep.
I can master them both if my grip holds out,
If the rocks bring succor and lend support,
Strength in the struggle. Ask me my name!

Book-Moth

A moth ate a word. To me it seemed
A marvelous thing when I learned the wonder
That a worm had swallowed, in darkness stolen,
The song of a man, his glorious sayings,
A great man's strength; and the thieving guest
Was no whit the wiser for the words it ate.

Cuckoo

In former days my father and mother
Abandoned me dead, lacking breath
Or life or being. Then one began,
A kinswoman kind, to care for and love me;
Covered me with her clothing, wrapped me in her raiment
With the same affection she felt for her own;

* Exeter Book *Riddles* 16, 47, 9, 85, 27, 14, 21, 5, 7, 2–3.

Until by the law of my life's shaping
Under alien bosom I quickened with breath.
My foster mother fed me thereafter
Until I grew sturdy and strengthened for flight.
Then of her dear ones, of daughters and sons,
She had the fewer for what she did.

Fish in River

My house is not quiet, I am not loud;
But for us God fashioned our fate together.
I am the swifter, at times the stronger,
My house more enduring, longer to last.
At times I rest; my dwelling still runs;
Within it I lodge as long as I live.
Should we two be severed, my death is sure.

Honey-Mead

I am valued by men, fetched from afar,
Gleaned on the hill-slopes, gathered in groves,
In dale and on down. All day through the air
Wings bore me aloft, and brought me with cunning
Safe under roof. Men steeped me in vats.
Now I have power to pummel and bind,
To cast to the earth, old man and young.
Soon he shall find who reaches to seize me,
Pits force against force, that he's flat on the ground,
Stripped of his strength if he cease not his folly,
Loud in his speech, but of power despoiled
To manage his mind, his hands or his feet.
Now ask me my name, who can bind men on earth
And lay fools low in the light of day.

Horn

Time was when I was weapon and warrior;
Now the young hero hoods me with gold,
And twisted silver. At times men kiss me.
At times I speak and summon to battle
Loyal companions. At times a courser
Bears me o'er marchland. At times a ship
Bears me o'er billows, brightly adorned.
At times a fair maiden fills me with breath;
At times hard and headless I lie on the board,
Bereft of beauty. At times I hang
Winsome on wall, richly embellished,
Where revelers drink. At times a warrior
Bears me on horse, a battle adornment,
And I swallow, bright-shining, the breath from his bosom.
At times with my strains I summon the heroes
Proudly to wine. At times I win back
Spoil from the spoiler, with sounding voice
Put foemen to flight. Now ask what I'm called.

Plow

My beak is bent downward, I burrow below;
I grub in the ground and go as he guides,
My gray, old master, foe of the forest.
Stoop-shouldered my warder walks at my back,
Fares through the field, urges and drives me,
Sows in my track as I sniff along.
Fetched from the wood, cunningly fitted,
Brought in a wagon, I have wondrous skill.
As I go my way on one side is green;
On the other side plain is my dark path.
Set through my back hangs a cunning spike;
Another fixed forward is fast to my head.
What I tear with my teeth falls to one side,
If he handles me right who is my ruler.

Shield

A lonely wanderer, wounded with iron,
I am smitten with war-blades, sated with strife,
Worn with the sword-edge; I have seen many battles,
Much hazardous fighting, oft without hope
Of comfort or help in the carnage of war
Ere I perish and fall in the fighting of men.
The leavings of hammers, the handwork of smiths,
Batter and bite me, hard-edged and sharp;
The brunt of battle I am doomed to endure.
In all the folk-stead no leech could I find
With wort or simple to heal my wounds;
But day and night with the deadly blows
The marks of the war-blades double and deepen.

Wild Swan

My attire is noiseless when I tread the earth,
Rest in its dwellings or ride its waters.
At times my pinions and the lofty air
Lift me high o'er the homes of men,
And the strength of the clouds carries me far
High over the folk. My feathers gay
Sound and make music, singing shrill,
When no longer I linger by field or flood,
But soar in air, a wandering spirit.

Wind

At times I resort, beyond man's discerning,
Under surging billows to seek the bottom,
The ocean depths. Then the sea is shaken,
Convulsed with foam, and the whale-flood rages
In giant uproar. The ocean streams
Beat on the shore and batter the slopes
With rock and sand, with seaweed and wave.

As I struggle and strain in the ocean depths
I shake the land and the vast sea-bottom.
From my watery covering I cannot forth
Till He grant me freedom Who guides my way
On every journey. O wise of wit,
Tell who can draw me from ocean depths
When the seas grow still and the waves are calm
Which formerly covered and cloaked me over.
Closely at times my master confines me,
Forces me under the fruitful plain,
The earth's broad bosom, and holds me at bay,
Pens my strength in prison and darkness
Where the earth sits heavy and hard on my back!
Out of that bondage escape is barred,
But I wrench and rock the dwellings of men.
The halls horn-gabled totter and topple
And over the households the high walls shake;
The air seems still, and the sea is silent,
Until from bondage I burst my way
As He may guide Who in the beginning
Laid fetters upon me and bitter bonds;
I may not ever escape from His power
Who governs my going.
At times from above
I must rouse the waters and stir the waves
And dash on its beaches the flint-gray flood.
The foaming breakers fight with the sea-wall,
Hills of water heave dark on the deep;
Each follows other in dusky track,
Churning combers that batter the cliffs
At the edge of the land. On ship is uproar,
Shouting of sailors. The steep stone cliffs
Await the sea-war, the crashing of waves,
As the dashing billows buffet the headlands.
On ship is dread of the perilous strife
Lest the ocean bear it with its burden of souls
To the dreadful hour when foaming it drives,

Bereft of rudder, stripped of sailors,
On the shouldering surges. Then terror shall come
In stormy might on the sons of men
Which is greater than I. Whose power shall still it?
At times I rush through the clouds that ride me,
Black vessels of rain, and scatter them far;
At times I join and gather them in.
The greatest of tumults resounds over cities,
The loudest of thunders, when cloud meets cloud
Edge against edge. Then swift over men
The swart shapes sweat bright fire and flame,
And dark o'er the hosts with the greatest of dins
The thunder breaks. Then the battling hosts
From their bosoms shed dark showers of rain,
Water from the womb. They fight their way on,
Dread troop on troop, and the terror grows,
Dismay of men and fear in the cities,
When the stalking specters shoot forth their fire.
The fool then fears not the deadly arrows,
But he perishes surely if God in sooth
Out of the rain and the roar of the whirlwind
Looses against him a flying bolt.
But few survive whom the swift foe strikes,
Reaches with weapon. I rouse this strife
When I rush in might with a meeting of clouds
O'er the breast of torrents; then burst with a roar
The cloud-troops on high. Then low under heaven
I bow to earth and load on my back,
At the word of my Lord, the burden I carry.
And so at times, a powerful slave,
I work under earth; at times I descend
Under surges of ocean; at times from above
I rouse the sea-streams; at times I mount up
And whirl the cloud-drift. Widely I fare
Strong and swift! Say what I'm called;
Who it is rouses me when I may not rest;
Who it is stays me when again I'm still.

Cotton MS. *Maxims*

King must rule kingdom. Cities are seen from afar,
Cunning handwork of giants who inhabit this earth,
Wondrous work of wallstones. Wind is swiftest in air,
Thunder at times is loudest. Great are the glories of Christ.
Wyrd is mightiest, winter is coldest,
Spring is frostiest, longest cold;
Summer is sunniest, sun is hottest,
Autumn most glorious giving to man
The fruits of the year that God brings forth.
Truth is clearest, treasure is dearest,
Gold most precious, age most wise;
Years make prudent who suffers long.
Woe is close clinging; clouds drift by.
Good companions encourage a prince
To glory in battle and giving of gifts.
Eorl must have courage; edge against helm
Survives the sword-play. Hawk on glove
The wild one waits. Wolf in the forest,
Beastly lone-goer. Boar in the wood,
Mighty of tusk. Good man at home
Harvests renown. Spear for the hand
Garnished with gold. Gem for the ring
Ample and wide. Stream in the waves
Shall mix with the sea. Mast for the ship,
The sailyard fastened. Sword on lap,
A lordly blade. In mound dragon bideth,
Old guarder of gold. Fish in water
Must spawn its kind. King in the hall
Must hand out rings. Bear on the heath
Roams old and fierce. River from hills
Flows down flood-gray. Army must be gathered,
A band of the brave. Faith for an eorl,
Wisdom for man. Woods of the world
Must bud with blossoms. Hills of earth

Must gleam with green. God in heaven
Is judge of deeds. Door in the hall
Is mouth of the building. Boss on shield
Is the fingers' guard. Birds above
Soar in the air. In deep pool salmon
Swims with the trout. Showers from heaven
Mingled with wind sweep over the world.
Thief goes in darkness. Ghost on the fen
Is alone in the land. In secret a woman
Will haste to her friend if she has no wish
To prosper with husband, purchased with rings.
Sea shall be salt; water and air
Shall flow in floods around all lands.
Cattle on earth shall bear and bring forth.
Stars shine bright by the Maker's command.
Good against evil; youth against age;
Life against death; light against darkness;
Army against army; foe against foe;
Hostile with hostile shall always fight
Contending for land and avenging wrongs.
A wise man must ponder this world's strife;
Outlaw must hang, paying the price
That he wronged mankind.
God alone knows
Where the soul passes and all the spirits
Who after their death-days go before God.
They abide their judgment in the Father's bosom;
Their future fate is secret and hid;
God alone knows, the Saviour Father.
And none returns ever, hither under roof,
To tell men for truth of God's decree,
Or the home of the victor-folk, where He Himself dwells.

Exeter Book *Fates of Men**

Oft it befalls by the grace of God
That into this world woman and man
Bring child to birth. They dress it in colors,
Love it and train it till time shall come
When its limbs are sturdy and strong with life.
Father and mother carry and lead it,
Feed it and clothe it but God alone knows
What the years may give for the growing child!
To one it happens in the years of his youth
A woeful ending carries him off.
A wolf shall devour him, hoary heath-stepper,
And his mother shall mourn his going hence.
Little is this the lot of a man!
One hunger shall waste, one storm shall harry
One spear shall slay, one battle destroy.
One lives his life without light of eye,
Only hands for feeling. One feeble of foot,
Sick of sinew, shall moan his pain,
Afflicted in spirit and mourning his fate.
One in the forest from lofty tree
Wingless shall fall; he shall be in flight
Swinging in air till no longer he hangs
As fruit from the bough. He shall fall to earth,
Of soul bereft at the root of the tree.
His life is ended. Over far ways
One shall travel, finding his food,
Facing the perils of foreign soil,
Having few friends to offer him welcome,
Everywhere hated, unhappy at heart,
Everywhere finding misfortune and woe.
One shall swing on the stretching gallows
Dangling in death till the body breaks,

*lines 1–67; 93–8.

The bloody frame, and the black-coated raven
Picks at the eyeballs, plucks at the corpse.
Against the outrage his hands are helpless;
They may not defend from the winged foe.
Life is vanished, all feeling fled.
Stark and pallid he swings on the gallows,
Shrouded in death-mist, enduring his fate.
His name is accursed. In the funeral-fire
Flame shall afflict, red brands consume
One doomed and fated; his death shall be swift.
The woman shall weep as she sees the blaze,
The enveloping flame, devour her son.

From one on the mead-bench, a wine-sated man
A quarrelsome drunkard, the sharp-edged sword
Shall wrest away life; his words were too rash!
One at the beer-feast by cupbearer's hand
Grown foolish with mead, not curbing his mouth,
Shall lose his life in a wretched brawl,
Shorn of pleasure, suffering woe;
And men who describe the drunkard's debauch,
All shall call him a self-slain man.

But some shall in youth by the grace of God
Master misfortune, in later years
Have joyous heart and days of gladness,
Feasting with loved ones, possessing wealth
And all such treasure as man may hold.

So in diverse ways God deals His gifts
Unto every man through all the earth:
He decides, and settles, and makes decree,
Giving weal to one, woe to another. . . .
In wondrous wise the Warden of hosts
Throughout the world awards man's fate,
Deciding fortune for all on earth.
Therefore, let every man give Him Thanksgiving
For all that His mercy may allot for men.

Exeter Book *Maxims* *

Frost shall freeze; fire melt wood;
Earth give blossom; ice shall bridge
And roof the waters, wondrously lock
Earth's budding growth. One shall unbind
The fetters of frost, Almighty God.
Winter shall pass, fair weather return,
Sun-hot summer and restless sea.
Deep slow wave holds secret longest.
Holly shall be lighted; dead man's wealth
Among heirs divided. Honor is best!
King with wealth shall purchase his queen
With beakers and bracelets; both, from the first,
Shall be gracious in giving. In the lord must grow
Courage and war-might; the lady shall thrive
Beloved of her people, a keeper of counsel,
Light of heart and liberal-handed
With horses and treasure; at drinking of mead
Before the host she shall first give greeting
To the leader of warriors, to hand of her lord
First tendering cup; knowing wise counsel
To the good of both, house-owners together.
Ship shall be nailed, and buckler bound,
Linden shield light; loved one is welcome
To Frisian wife when his boat stands in.
His ship is come and her sailor home,
Her own food-winner. She welcomes him in,
Washes his garments stained by the sea,
Gives him new raiment. Sweet is the shore
To one whose longing is urged by love.
A wife should ever keep faith with her man;
But often she shames him with evil ways.
Many are steadfast, many are fickle

* Lines 71–106; 201–4.

Wooing strange men when their lords are away.
Often the sailor is long at sea;
But one must look for the loved one's coming
Awaiting the meeting one may not speed,
Till the time shall come that he turns again home,
Alive and hale, unless ocean trammel,
Or deep sea hold him with clutching hand. . . .
  Shield shall be ready, barb on shaft,
Edge on sword and point on spear!
Stout heart for hero, helm for the brave,
And ever for faint-heart scantest of hoards!

IV

CONTINENTAL TRADITION

CONTINENTAL TRADITION

Old English poetry affords evidence of the extent to which Continental tradition persisted in England. It is reflected, of course, in the Scandinavian backgrounds of *Beowulf*, in the poet's retelling of the legends of Sigemund and Finn, and in countless allusions to material of legend and chronicle scattered through the poem. It is found also in details of shorter poems like *Widsith* and *Deor's Lament*, and in the brief poetic fragments that deal with the material of the Waldere and Finnsburg stories.

The Tale of Sigemund in *Beowulf* is in one respect unique, for in Continental legend the great dragon-fight is fought, not by Sigemund, but by his son Sigurd. Moreover, the *Lay of Finn* inset in the poem has little direct relation to the *Finnsburg Fragment* where the theme is the heroic fighting for possession of the great hall. In the *Beowulf Lay* the theme is extended to the tragic issues involved in the bloody racial feud between Danes and Frisians.

Widsith and *Deor's Lament* are poems of minstrel life. Widsith, a strolling singer, tells of his travels, of the great rulers he has known, and the rich gifts he has received. But the allusions cover so many years that no actual Widsith could have visited all the heroic figures he names. Indeed it is a question whether the long "catalogue" of rulers and tribes was a part of the original poem. In many instances, the *Widsith* supplements names and allusions that occur in other Old English poems. Lines 45-49 mention the bitter feud between Danes and Heathobards outlined by Beowulf in his account of his Danish adventures.

The *Lament* of Deor, once court-singer of the Heodenings, tells of his displacement by the minstrel Heorrenda who had supplanted him in his lord's favor and succeeded to the "'landright" Deor once had held. The poem is in strophic arrangement, each strophe rehearsing historic instances of adversity and ending with the refrain: "That evil ended, so also may this!" As Weland and Beadohild, Theodoric and the subjects of Eormanric, had risen above misfortune, so may others also surmount adverse fate.

The two Old English fragments of the *Waldere* are very brief portions of a legend of Walther of Aquitaine. A tenth-century Latin text of this heroic tale, the *Waltharius*, is, except for the Old English fragments, the oldest of surviving versions. The first of the *Waldere* fragments contains a part of Hildegund's exhortation of Walther to do or die in the battle with Gunther. The second fragment includes Walther's challenge of Gunther to come and take, if he can, the corselet that Walther had from his father. If one can judge from these spirited speeches, the *Waldere* in its entirety may well have been an excellent example of the Germanic heroic tale in Old English verse.

Deor's Lament

Weland knew fully affliction and woe,
Hero unflinching enduring distress;
Had for companionship heart-break and longing,
Wintry exile and anguish of soul,
When Nithhad bound him, the better man,
Grimly constrained him with sinewy bonds.
That evil ended. So also may this!
Nor was brother's death to Beadohild
A sorrow as deep as her own sad plight,
When she knew the weight of the child in her womb,
But little could know what her lot might be.
That evil ended. So also may this!
Many have heard of the rape of Hild,
Of her father's affection and infinite love,
Whose nights were sleepless with sorrow and grief.
That evil ended. So also may this!
For thirty winters Theodoric held,
As many have known, the Mæring's stronghold.
That evil ended. So also may this!
We have heard of Eormanric's wolf-like ways,
Widely ruling the realm of the Goths;
Grim was his menace, and many a man,
Weighted with sorrow and presage of woe,
Wished that the end of his kingdom were come.
That evil ended. So also may this!
He who knows sorrow, despoiled of joys,
Sits heavy of mood; to his heart it seemeth
His measure of misery meeteth no end.
Yet well may he think how oft in this world
The wise Lord varies His ways to men,
Granting wealth and honor to many an eorl,
To others awarding a burden of woe.

And so I can sing of my own sad plight
Who long stood high as the Heodenings' bard,
Deor my name, dear to my lord.
Mild was my service for many a winter,
Kindly my king till Heorrenda came
Skillful in song and usurping the land-right
Which once my gracious lord granted to me.
That evil ended. So also may this!

Widsith, the Minstrel *

Widsith spoke, his word-hoard unlocked,
Who most had traveled of men on earth
Among many peoples, and prospered in hall
With splendid treasure. His forebears sprang
From the Myrging tribe. In his earliest travels
With Ealhild he went, fair weaver of peace,
From the East out of Angle to Eormanric's home,
Who was prince of the Goths, fierce breaker of pledges.
Many a tale he told of his travels:
"Much have I learned of the rulers of men!
A prince must live by custom and law,
Each after other ruling the realm,
Who wishes his power to prosper and thrive.
Of them was Hwala a while the best,
And Alexander greatest of all
Of the race of men; he prospered most
Of all I have heard of over the earth.
Attila ruled the Huns, Eormanric the Goths,
Becca the Banings, Gifica the Burgundians;
Caesar ruled the Greeks, Caelic the Finns,
Hagena the Holmrygir, Heoden the Glomman;
Witta ruled the Swabians, Wada the Hælsings,
Meaca the Myrgings, Mearchealf the Hundings;
Theodoric ruled the Franks, Thyle the Rondings,
Breca the Brondings, Billing the Wernas;
Oswine ruled the Eowas, Gefwulf the Jutes,
Finn, son of Folcwalda, the Frisian folk.
Sighere longest governed the Sea Danes;
Hnæf ruled the Hocings, Helm the Wulfings. . . .
"I have fared through many a foreign land

* *Widsith* 1–29; 50–58; 70–74; 88–108; 135–43.

Over spacious earth, knowing weal and woe,
Bereft of my kinsmen, far from my folk,
Widely wandering over the world.
Many a song and many a story
I can tell in the mead-hall, recounting to men
How princes and nobles graced me with gifts.
I was with the Huns, and with the Hrethgoths,
With Swedes I was, and with Geats, and with South-Danes. . . .
"I was in Italy also with Ælfwine
Who of all mankind as ever I heard
Had the easiest hand in the earning of praise,
And the readiest heart in the giving of rings,
The shining jewels, Eadwine's son. . . .
"I was with Eormanric, and all the while
The king of the Goths was gracious and kind.
He gave me a ring, the ruler of cities,
Worth six hundred sceats counted in cost
Of shilling pieces of smelted gold.
To Eadgils I gave it, my gracious lord,
To requite his kindness when home I came.
For the lord of the Myrgings had granted me land,
The holding and home of my father before me.
"And Ealhild also gave me a ring,
The fair folk-queen, the daughter of Eadwine.
To many a people her praise I published
Whenever in song my task was to tell
Of a gold-decked queen most kind under heaven,
Best and most gracious in giving of gifts.
There Scilling and I in echoing strains
Before our dear lord lifted our songs.
Loud to the harp the lay resounded;
And many a noble who knew aright
Said he had never heard better song." . . .
Widely they wander, as Fate may guide,
The strolling singers who roam the world

Telling their need, returning their thanks,
And always finding, or south or north,
Some great one skilled in knowledge of song
Who is open-handed in giving of gifts,
Who seeks for honor and strives for fame
Till all things vanish, light and life
Passing together. He who earns praise
Has under heaven the greatest glory.

The Tale of Sigemund *

Old tales were told of Sigemund's daring,
War-deeds of the Wælsing, his wanderings wide,
Much of unknown, the merciless feuds
The sons of men no longer remembered,
Save Fitela only, as uncle to nephew
Had told these tales when they fought together,
Battle-comrades in bitter fight.
Many a monster they slew with the sword.
After Sigemund's death his glory increased
For the keen in battle had killed the Worm,
The treasure-guarder. Beneath gray rock
The valiant hero had ventured alone
On the fearful deed. Nor was Fitela with him.
To him it was granted his good sword pierced
The wondrous Worm till it stood in the wall,
The lordly iron. The Dragon died.
The hero's valor had won the treasure,
The hoard to enjoy as his heart might wish.
He loaded his sea-boat, bore to its bosom
Shining treasure, the son of Wæls.
The surge of its fire consumed the Worm.
He was of heroes most famous afar
For daring deeds, the defender of fighters.
He prospered greatly long ago!

* *Beowulf* 874–900.

The Lay of Finn *

Then Hrothgar's minstrel rehearsed the lay
Of the sons of Finn when the slaughter befell them:
Hnæf of the Scyldings, the Half-Dane hero,
Was doomed to death in the Frisian fight.
Nor could Hildeburh praise the faith of the Jutes!
She was blameless, shorn of brothers and sons
In the play of shields, deprived of beloved
Fated and fallen, wounded with spears.
Her heart was heavy. Not for little Hoc's daughter
Mourned their death at the dawning of day
When she saw under sky the slaughter of kinsmen
Where once she had known life's fairest delights.
  War laid them low, the thanes of Finn,
Save only a few. Nor could he fight Hengest
Or harry his host; and they offered a truce:
A hall and high-seat, a sharing of rights
With the sons of the Jutes; and that Folcwalda's son
Would honor the Danes, in the giving of gifts,
With rings and gold as he gave to the Frisians
To gladden their hearts on benches in hall.
Both trusted the terms of the truce. And Finn
Swore oaths to Hengest forceful and firm
He would rule his remnant by councils' decree;
And that no man ever by act or by word
Would break the truce, or mention with malice
That they who were lordless were fated to follow
The lord who had killed their former king;
And if ever a Frisian should fan the feud
With insolent speech the sword would avenge it.
  Then the pyre was prepared, gold drawn from the hoard,

* *Beowulf* 1066–1159.

And the Scylding leader was laid on the bier.
In the funeral flame was easily seen
Blood-stained byrny and golden swine,
Gilded boar-helm hard from the hammer,
And many a warrior fated with wounds
And fallen in battle. Hildeburh bade
That her son be laid on the bier of Hnæf
And his body burned at his uncle's shoulder.
The lady lamented with mournful dirge.
The hero was placed on the funeral pyre;
The greatest of bale-fires rolled with a roar
To the skies above at the burial barrow.
Then heads were melted and wounds gaped wide;
Blood flowed, and flame, most greedy of spirits,
Swallowed all battle had taken of both their peoples.
Their glory was gone. The warriors went to their homes,
Bereft of friends, returning to Friesland
To city and stronghold. But Hengest remained
Abiding unhappy with Finn. Though he longed for home,
He could not sail on the sea his ring-stemmed ship.
The billows boiled with storm and strove with the wind;
Winter locked ocean with bonds of ice,
Till a new Spring shone on the dwellings of men,
As still it does, the sunny and shining days
That ever observe their season. The winter was gone
And fair was the bosom of earth. Then the exile
Longed to be gone, the guest from his dwelling.
But his mind was more on revenge than on sailing the sea,
Assault on the Jutes and a storming with sword.
He spurned it not when Hunlafing laid in his lap
His battle-flasher, the best of blades.
Well known was its war-edge to men of the Jutes!
Then death by the sword befell Finn, the fierce-hearted,
When Oslaf and Guthlaf brooded on the grim attack,
After the sea-journey sorrow and weight of woe,

And they could not bridle the fury within their breasts.
The hall was strewn with bodies and red with blood;
Finn was killed, the king with his men,
And the queen was taken. The Scyldings carried to ship
All the wealth of the king, such jewels and gems
As they found in the home of Finn. And the fairest of women
They bore over sea-paths back to the Danes
Back to her home, and her own dear people.

The Battle of Finnsburg

. . ."are the horns of the hall on fire?"
Then Hnæf made answer, the battle-young king:
"This is no dawn from the East, nor flying dragon,
Nor fire burning the horns of this hall,
But men in armor; the eagle shall scream,
The gray wolf howl and the war-wood whistle,
Shield answer shaft. Now shines the moon
Through scudding cloud. Dire deeds are come
Bringing hard battle and bitter strife.
Awake, my warriors, seize your shields;
Fight like men in the front of battle;
Be bold of mood, be mindful of valor!"
Then sprang up many a gold-decked thane,
Girding on sword. The great-hearted warriors,
Sigeferth and Eaha, drew their swords,
Springing to one door; Ordlaf and Guthlaf
Guarded the other while Hengest himself
Followed them close. Garulf urged Guthere
In the first onset not so freely
At the door of the hall to hazard his life,
Where the bold in battle would wrench it away.
But the brave-hearted hero, for all to hear,
Called to know who was holding the door?
"Sigeferth is my name (said he); I am prince of the Secgas
A wide-known wanderer; I have borne many blows
In many fierce battles. At my hand you can have
Whatever you wish to have from me."
Then in the hall was the sound of slaughter,
Boat-shaped shield upraised by the brave.
Bucklers burst; hall-boards resounded;
Till Garulf in fighting was first to fall,
The son of Guthlaf, with many a good man,
Bodies of dying. Swarthy and dark
The ravens were circling. There was flashing of swords

As if all Finnsburg were blazing with fire.
  Never have I heard of worthier warriors
Who bore themselves better in brunt of war,
Or of finer service more fitly paid
Than those young heroes rendered to Hnæf.
Five days they fought and none of them fell,
His faultless comrades, and they held the doors.
  Then a wounded warrior turned him away,
Said his byrny was broken his war-gear weak,
His helmet pierced. The prince of the people
Asked how the warriors survived their wounds,
Or which of the young men. . . .

Waldere 1 *

. . . heard him gladly.
"Weland's work surely can never weaken
For any man who can hold the hard blade,
Wield the sword, Mimming. Often in war
Wounded and bloody man after man
Fell in the fray. Now let not thy strength,
Soldier of Attila, or thy valor fail.
"Now the day has come when thou shalt accomplish
One of two: either lose thy life,
Or win long fame, O Ælfhere's son,
Among all mankind. Not at all, my beloved,
Can I say that ever in play of swords
I saw you shamefully shun the battle,
Or turn to the wall to protect your life,
Though many a hard blade hacked at your byrny.
But always further you forced the fighting
Time beyond measure; I feared for your fate
Lest all too boldly you pressed to the battle,
The bloody encounter in clash of war.
"Now honor your name with deeds of note
While God is gracious and grants you strength.
Fear not for the blade! The best of weapons
Was surely given to save us both.
With its edge you shall beat down Guthhere's boast
Who wickedly started this bitter strife,
Refused the sword, and the shining casket,
And wealth of jewels. With never a gem
He shall leave the battle, return to his lord,
His ancient homeland, or here shall he sleep
If he . . ."

* Fragment 1, 1–32.

Waldere 2 *

Waldere addressed him, the warrior brave;
He held in his hand his comfort in battle,
War-blade in his grip, and uttered these words:
"Lo! grimly you hoped Burgundian lord,
That the hand of Hagen would help in the fray
And hinder my fighting; try and take, if you dare,
Battle-worn though I be, my good gray byrny.
Here it lies on my shoulders, shining with gold,
Ælfhere's heirloom of ample front,
A peerless corselet for prince's wear
When hand guards body and frame from the foe!
It fails me not when the false and unfriendly
Renew their tricks, and attack me with swords
As ye have done."

* Fragment 2, 11–24.

Charm for a Sudden Stitch

(*For a sudden stitch: feverfew, and the red nettle that grows into the house, and plantain; boil in butter.*)

Loud were they, loud, as they rode o'er the hill;
Fierce was their mood as they rode through the land;
Shield thee now and be healed of this hurt;
Out little spear, if in here it be!
I lifted up linden, my shining shield,
When the mighty women mustered their strength,
And sped against me their screaming spears.
Back again I'll give them another,
A flying arrow full in the front;
Out little spear, if in here it be!
Sat a smith a little knife shaping,
Most cutting of irons, wondrous keen;
Out little spear, if in here it be!
Six smiths sat slaughter-spears shaping;
Out spear! Be not in, spear!
If here within be a whit of iron,
The work of witches, it shall melt away.
Be thou shot in fell, or shot in flesh,
Or shot in blood, or shot in bone,
Or shot in limb be thy life unscathed!
Were it shot of Esa, or shot of elves,
Or shot of hags, now will I help thee!
This—to heal Esa-shot; This—to heal elf-shot;
This—to heal hag-shot; So will I help thee!
Fly, witch, to the wood; healed be this hurt!
So help thee the Lord!

Charm for Unfruitful Land

Erce, Erce, Erce, Mother of earth,
May the All-Wielder, Lord Eternal,
Give flourishing acres of sprouting shoots,
Acres bountiful bringing to harvest
Tall stalks and shining growth,
Acres of broad harvest of barley,
Acres of white harvest of wheat,
And all the harvests of earth!
May Eternal God and His saints in heaven
Defend earth's growth from every foe
That it may be shielded from every evil,
And every sorcery sowed through the land.
Now I pray the All-Wielder who shaped the world
That there be no woman so wagging of tongue,
Nor any man so cunning of craft,
That may ever pervert the words thus spoken!

(*Then take the plough, and turn the first furrow, and say:*)

Be healed, O Earth, O Mother of men,
Be hale and growing by grace of God:
Be filled with food for the use of men!

(*Then take meal of every kind and bake a loaf as broad as the inside of the hand, and knead it with milk and with holy water, and lay it under the first furrow. Then say:*)

Acre grow full with food for men
Brightly blowing. Be thou blessed
In the name of the Holy One, Maker of heaven,
And Maker of earth whereon we live.
May God, Who made ground, grant sprouting gifts
That each kind of grain may grow for men.

V

BEOWULF'S LAST BATTLE

BEOWULF'S LAST BATTLE

Of unknown authorship, the *Beowulf* is the outstanding poetic achievement of its age. It is a poem of cultivated craftsmanship and Christian spirit. Sophisticated rather than primitive, its style suggests the influence of literary tradition. Its lines move with an epic dignity of speech and action which may reflect a debt to Vergil in an age when the *Aeneid* was well known to scholars.

The material of the poem is largely Scandinavian. Beowulf's slaying of the hall-haunting Grendel and the troll-wife, his mother, has analogues in various versions of the Continental "Bear's Son" folk-tale. Names of early Swedish kings, mentioned in *Beowulf*, correspond to names in the *Ynglinga Tal*. Incidents relating to the ruling house of the Danes have their analogues in the *Skjoldungasaga*. Woven into this material are references to the savage feuds of the Continental tribes, the Danes and Frisians, Danes and Heathobards, Geats and Swedes.

It is not possible to trace the dragon-fight in *Beowulf* to specific sources or analogues. However, the guarding of burial treasure by a dragon is in accord with the nature of dragons as set forth in the *Gnomic Verses* of the Cotton MS: "The dragon bideth in the grave-mound, old guarder of gold." The treasure buried in the *Beowulf* grave-mound is described in a vivid passage, 2232-70, that is worthy of comparison with the elegiac lines of *The Wanderer*, and *The Ruin*.

The fire-dragon of *Beowulf*, roused by the theft of a flagon from its hoard, ravaged the kingdom with flame. Beowulf and eleven followers went out against him. But Beowulf's comrades, terrified at the dragon's first onset, fled from the battle. Only the youthful Wiglaf remained to fight beside his lord, and his curse upon the cowards is one of the finest expressions of *comitatus* loyalty in Old English verse. In its third rush the dragon fastened its fangs in Beowulf's throat. The king had received his death-wound and his fast failing strength barely sufficed, with Wiglaf's help, to strike down the beast.

There is a climactic grandeur in the final scenes of *Beowulf* which illustrates well the author's poetic skill. He describes no popular rejoicing over the killing of the dragon, or the recovery of the rich treasure hoard. The dragon's huge carcass is tumbled over the cliff-edge into the sea, and the treasure is reburied in Beowulf's barrow. An immeasurable disaster had befallen the Geats. Beowulf had ruled them long with strength and wisdom, a settler of ancient feuds, a preserver of peace. The Messenger who brought the news of his death rehearsed the bloody battle against the Swedes at Ravenswood, and chanted his foreboding of evil days to come. A shadow of doom darkened over the people. The old order was ending with the funeral flames and the sound of a people's sorrow for the passing of a great king.

The Fire-Dragon and the Treasure *

It later befell in the years that followed
After Hygelac sank in the surges of war,
And the sword slew Heardred under his shield
When the Battle-Scylfings, those bitter fighters,
Invaded the land of the victor-folk
Overwhelming Hereric's nephew in war,
That the kingdom came into Beowulf's hand.
For fifty winters he governed it well,
Aged and wise with the wisdom of years,
Till a fire-drake flying in darkness of night
Began to ravage and work his will.
On the upland heath he guarded a hoard,
A stone barrow lofty. Under it lay
A path concealed from the sight of men.
There a thief broke in on the heathen treasure,
Laid hand on a flagon all fretted with gold,
As the dragon discovered, though cozened in sleep
By the pilferer's cunning. The people soon found
That the mood of the dragon was roused to wrath!
Not at all with intent, of his own free will,
Did he ravish the hoard, who committed the wrong;
But in dire distress the thrall of a thane,
A guilty fugitive fleeing the lash,
He forced his way in. There a horror befell him!
Yet the wretched exile escaped from the dragon,
Swift in retreat when the terror arose.
A flagon he took. There, many such treasures
Lay heaped in that earth-hall where the owner of old
Had carefully hidden the precious hoard,
The countless wealth of a princely clan.
Death came upon them in days gone by

* *Beowulf* 2200–2354.

And he who lived longest, the last of his line,
Guarding the treasure and grieving for friend,
Deemed it his lot that a little while only
He too might hold that ancient hoard.
A barrow new-built near the ocean billows
Stood cunningly fashioned beneath the cliff;
Into the barrow the ring-warden bore
The princely treasure, the precious trove
Of golden wealth, and these words he spoke:
"Keep thou, O Earth, what men could not keep,
This costly treasure —it came from thee!
Baleful slaughter has swept away,
Death in battle, the last of my blood;
They have lived their lives; they have left the mead-hall.
Now I have no one to wield the sword,
No one to polish the plated cup,
The precious flagon; the host is fled.
The hard-forged helmet fretted with gold
Shall be stripped of its inlay; the burnishers sleep
Whose charge was to brighten the battle-masks.
Likewise the corselet that countered in war
Mid clashing of bucklers the bite of the sword—
Corselet and warrior decay into dust;
Mailed coat and hero are moveless and still.
No mirth of gleewood, no music of harp,
No good hawk swinging in flight through the hall;
No swift steed stamps in the castle yard;
Death has ravished an ancient race."
So sad of mood he bemoaned his sorrow,
Lonely and sole survivor of all,
Restless by day and wretched by night
Till the clutch of death caught at his heart.
Then the goodly treasure was found unguarded
By the venomous dragon enveloped in flame,
The old naked night-foe flying in darkness,
Haunting the barrows; a bane that brings

A fearful dread to the dwellers of earth.
His wont is to hunt out a hoard under ground
And guard heathen gold, growing old with the years.
But no whit for that is his fortune more fair!
  For three hundred winters this waster of peoples
Held the huge treasure-hall under the earth
Till the robber aroused him to anger and rage,
Stole the rich beaker and bore to his master,
Imploring his lord for a compact of peace.
So the hoard was robbed and its riches plundered;
To the wretch was granted the boon that he begged;
And his liege-lord first had view of the treasure,
The ancient work of the men of old.
  Then the worm awakened and war was kindled,
The rush of the monster along the rock,
When the fierce one found the tracks of the foe;
He had stepped too close in his stealthy cunning
To the dragon's head. But a man undoomed
May endure with ease disaster and woe
If he has His favor who wields the world.
Swiftly the fire-drake sought through the plain
The man who wrought him this wrong in his sleep.
Inflamed and savage he circled the mound,
But the waste was deserted; no man was in sight.
  The worm's mood was kindled to battle and war;
Time and again he returned to the barrow
Seeking the treasure-cup. Soon he was sure
That a man had plundered the precious gold.
Enraged and restless the hoard-warden waited
The gloom of evening. The guard of the mound
Was swollen with anger; the fierce one resolved
To requite with fire the theft of the cup.
Then the day was sped as the worm desired;
Lurking no longer within his wall
He sallied forth surrounded with fire,
Encircled with flame. For the folk of the land

The beginning was dread as the ending was grievous
That came so quickly upon their lord.
  Then the baleful dragon belched fire and flame,
Burned the bright dwellings; the glow of the blaze
Filled hearts with horror. The hostile flier
Was minded to leave there nothing alive.
From near and from far the war of the dragon,
The might of the monster, was widely revealed
So that all could see how the ravaging scather
Hated and humbled the Geatish folk.
Then he hastened back ere the break of dawn
To his secret den and the spoil of gold.
He had compassed the land with a flame of fire,
A blaze of burning; he trusted the wall,
The sheltering mound, and the strength of his might.
But his trust betrayed him! The terrible news
Was brought to Beowulf, told for a truth,
That his home was consumed in the surges of fire,
The goodly dwelling and throne of the Geats.
  The heart of the hero was heavy with anguish,
The greatest of sorrows; in his wisdom he weened
He had grievously angered the Lord Everlasting,
Blamefully broken the ancient law.
Dark thoughts stirred in his surging bosom,
Welled in his breast, as was not his wont.
The flame of the dragon had leveled the fortress,
The people's stronghold washed by the wave.
But the king of warriors, prince of the Weders,
Exacted an ample revenge for it all.
The lord of warriors and leader of eorls
Bade work him of iron a wondrous shield,
Knowing full well that wood could not serve him
Nor linden defend him against the flame.
The stalwart hero was doomed to suffer
The destined end of his days on earth;
Likewise the worm, though for many a winter

He had held his watch o'er the wealth of the hoard.
  The ring-prince scorned to assault the dragon
With a mighty army, or host of men.
He feared not the combat, nor counted of worth
The might of the worm, his courage and craft,
Since often aforetime, beset in the fray,
He had safely issued from many an onset,
Many a combat and, crowned with success,
Purged of evil the hall of Hrothgar
And crushed out Grendel's loathsome kin. . . .

Beowulf and Wiglaf Slay the Dragon *

For the last time Beowulf uttered his boast:
"I came in safety through many a conflict
In the days of my youth; and now even yet,
Old as I am, I will fight this feud,
Do manful deeds, if the dire destroyer
Will come from his cavern to meet my sword."
The king for the last time greeted his comrades,
Bold helmet-bearers and faithful friends:
"I would bear no sword nor weapon to battle
With the evil worm, if I knew how else
I could close with the fiend, as I grappled with Grendel
From the worm I look for a welling of fire,
A belching of venom, and therefore I bear
Shield and byrny. Not one foot's space
Will I flee from the monster, the ward of the mound.
It shall fare with us both in the fight at the wall
As Fate shall allot, the lord of mankind.
Though bold in spirit, I make no boast
As I go to fight with the flying serpent.
Clad in your corselets and trappings of war,
By the side of the barrow abide you to see
Which of us twain may best after battle
Survive his wounds. Not yours the adventure,
Nor the mission of any, save mine alone,
To measure his strength with the monstrous dragon
And play the part of a valiant eorl.
By deeds of daring I'll gain the gold
Or death in battle shall break your lord."
Then the stalwart rose with his shield upon him,
Bold under helmet, bearing his sark
Under the stone-cliff; he trusted the strength
Of his single might. Not so does a coward!

* *Beowulf* 2510–2614; 2631–2711.

He who survived through many a struggle,
Many a combat and crashing of troops,
Saw where a stone-arch stood by the wall
And a gushing stream broke out from the barrow.
Hot with fire was the flow of its surge,
Nor could any abide near the hoard unburned,
Nor endure its depths, for the flame of the dragon.
Then the lord of the Geats in the grip of his fury
Gave shout of defiance; the strong-heart stormed.
His voice rang out with the rage of battle,
Resounding under the hoary stone.
Hate was aroused; the hoard-warden knew
'Twas the voice of a man. No more was there time
To sue for peace; the breath of the serpent,
A blast of venom, burst from the rock.
The ground resounded; the lord of the Geats
Under the barrow swung up his shield
To face the dragon; the coiling foe
Was gathered to strike in the deadly strife.
The stalwart hero had drawn his sword,
His ancient heirloom of tempered edge;
In the heart of each was fear of the other!
The shelter of kinsmen stood stout of heart
Under towering shield as the great worm coiled;
Clad in his war-gear he waited the rush.
In twisting folds the flame-breathing dragon
Sped to its fate. The shield of the prince
For a lesser while guarded his life and his body
Than heart had hoped. For the first time then
It was not his portion to prosper in war;
Fate did not grant him glory in battle!
Then lifted his arm the lord of the Geats
And smote the worm with his ancient sword
But the brown edge failed as it fell on bone,
And cut less deep than the king had need
In his sore distress. Savage in mood
The ward of the barrow countered the blow

With a blast of fire; wide sprang the flame.
The ruler of Geats had no reason to boast;
His unsheathed iron, his excellent sword,
Had weakened as it should not, had failed in the fight.
It was no easy journey for Ecgtheow's son
To leave this world and against his will
Find elsewhere a dwelling! So every man shall
In the end give over this fleeting life.
Not long was the lull. Swiftly the battlers
Renewed their grapple. The guard of the hoard
Grew fiercer in fury. His venomous breath
Beat in his breast. Enveloped in flame
The folk-leader suffered a sore distress.
No succoring band of shoulder-companions,
No sons of warriors aided him then
By valor in battle. They fled to the forest
To save their lives; but a sorrowful spirit
Welled in the breast of one of the band.
The call of kinship can never be stilled
In the heart of a man who is trusty and true.
His name was Wiglaf, Weohstan's son,
A prince of the Scylfings, a peerless thane,
Ælfhere's kinsman; he saw his king
Under his helmet smitten with heat.
He thought of the gifts which his lord had given,
The wealth and the land of the Wægmunding line
And all the folk-rights his father had owned;
Nor could he hold back, but snatched up his buckler,
His linden shield and his ancient sword,
Heirloom of Eanmund, Ohthere's son,
Whom Weohstan slew with the sword in battle,
Wretched and friendless and far from home. . . .
Wiglaf spoke in sorrow of soul,
With bitter reproach rebuking his comrades:
"I remember the time, as we drank in the mead-hall,
When we swore to our lord who bestowed these rings
That we would repay for the war-gear and armor,

The hard swords and helmets, if need like this
Should ever befall him. He chose us out
From all the host for this high adventure,
Deemed us worthy of glorious deeds,
Gave me these treasures, regarded us all
As high-hearted bearers of helmet and spear—
Though our lord himself, the shield of his people,
Thought single-handed to finish this feat,
Since of mortal men his measure was most
Of feats of daring and deeds of fame.
"Now is the day that our lord has need
Of the strength and courage of stalwart men.
Let us haste to succor his sore distress
In the horrible heat and the merciless flame.
God knows I had rather the fire should enfold
My body and limbs with my gold-friend and lord.
Shameful it seems that we carry our shields
Back to our homes ere we harry the foe
And ward the life of the Weder king.
Full well I know it is not his due
That he alone, of the host of the Geats,
Should suffer affliction and fall in the fight.
One helmet and sword, one byrny and shield,
Shall serve for us both in the storm of strife."
Then Wiglaf dashed through the deadly reek
In his battle-helmet to help his lord.
Brief were his words: "Beloved Beowulf,
Summon your strength, remember the vow
You made of old in the years of youth
Not to allow your glory to lessen
As long as you lived. With resolute heart,
And dauntless daring, defend your life
With all your force. I fight at your side!"
Once again the worm, when the words were spoken,
The hideous foe in a horror of flame,
Rushed in rage at the hated men.
Wiglaf's buckler was burned to the boss

In the billows of fire; his byrny of mail
Gave the young hero no help or defense.
But he stoutly pressed on under shield of his kinsman
When his own was consumed in the scorching flame.
  Then the king once more was mindful of glory,
Swung his great sword-blade with all his might
And drove it home on the dragon's head.
But Nægling broke, it failed in the battle,
The blade of Beowulf, ancient and gray.
It was not his lot that edges of iron
Could help him in battle; his hand was too strong,
Overtaxed, I am told, every blade with its blow.
Though he bore a wondrous hard weapon to war,
No whit the better was he thereby!
  A third time then the terrible scather,
The monstrous dragon inflamed with the feud,
Rushed on the king when the opening offered,
Fierce and flaming; fastened its fangs
In Beowulf's throat; he was bloodied with gore;
His life-blood streamed from the welling wound.
  As they tell the tale, in the king's sore need
His shoulder-companion showed forth his valor,
His craft and courage, and native strength.
To the head of the dragon he paid no heed,
Though his hand was burned as he helped his king.
A little lower the stalwart struck
At the evil beast, and his blade drove home
Plated and gleaming. The fire began
To lessen and wane. The king of the Weders
Summoned his wits; he drew the dagger
He wore on his corselet, cutting and keen
And slit asunder the worm with the blow.
So they felled the foe and wrought their revenge;
The kinsmen together had killed the dragon.
So a man should be when the need is bitter!
That was the last fight Beowulf fought;
That was the end of his work in the world.

Beowulf's Death *

The wound which the dragon had dealt him began
To swell and burn; and soon he could feel
The baneful venom inflaming his breast.
The wise, old warrior sank down by the wall
And stared at the work of the giants of old,
The arches of stone and the standing columns
Upholding the ancient earth-hall within.
His loyal thane, the kindest of comrades,
Saw Beowulf bloody and broken in war;
In his hands bore water and bathed his leader,
And loosened the helm from his dear lord's head.
Beowulf spoke, though his hurt was sore,
The wounds of battle grievous and grim.
Full well he weened that his life was ended,
And all the joy of his years on earth;
That his days were done, and Death most near:
"My armor and sword I would leave to my son
Had Fate but granted, born of my body,
An heir to follow me after I'm gone.
For fifty winters I've ruled this realm
And never a lord of a neighboring land
Dared strike with terror or seek with sword.
In my life I abode by the lot assigned,
Kept well what was mine, courted no quarrels,
Swore no false oaths. And now for all this
Though my hurt is grievous, my heart is glad.
When life leaves body, the Lord of mankind
Cannot lay to my charge the killing of kinsmen!
Go quickly, dear Wiglaf, to gaze on the gold
Beneath the hoar stone. The dragon lies still
In the sleep of death, despoiled of his hoard.
Make haste that my eyes may behold the treasure,

* *Beowulf* 2711–2891.

The gleaming jewels, the goodly store,
And, glad of the gold, more peacefully leave
The life and the realm I have ruled so long."
Then Weohstan's son, as they tell the tale,
Clad in his corselet and trappings of war,
Hearkened at once to his wounded lord.
Under roof of the barrow he broke his way.
Proud in triumph he stood by the seat,
Saw glittering jewels and gold on the ground,
The den of the dragon, the old dawn-flier,
And all the wonders along the walls.
Great bowls and flagons of bygone men
Lay all unburnished and barren of gems,
Many a helmet ancient and rusted,
Many an arm-ring cunningly wrought.
Treasure and gold, though hid in the ground,
Override man's wishes, hide them who will!
High o'er the hoard he beheld a banner,
Greatest of wonders, woven with skill,
All wrought of gold; its radiance lighted
The vasty ground and the glittering gems.
But no sign of the worm! The sword-edge had slain him.
As I've heard the tale, the hero unaided
Rifled those riches of giants of old,
The hoard in the barrow, and heaped in his arms
Beakers and platters, picked what he would
And took the banner, the brightest of signs.
The ancient sword with its edge of iron
Had slain the worm who watched o'er the wealth,
In the midnight flaming, with menace of fire
Protecting the treasure for many a year
Till he died the death. Then Wiglaf departed
In haste returning enriched with spoil.
He feared, and wondered if still he would find
The lord of the Weders alive on the plain,
Broken and weary and smitten with wounds.
With his freight of treasure he found the prince,

His dear lord, bloody and nigh unto death.
With water he bathed him till words broke forth
From the hoard of his heart and, aged and sad,
Beowulf spoke, as he gazed on the gold:
  "For this goodly treasure whereon I gaze
I give my thanks to the Lord of all,
To the Prince of glory, Eternal God,
Who granted me grace to gain for my people
Such dower of riches before my death.
I gave my life for this golden hoard.
Heed well the wants, the need of my people;
My hour is come, and my end is near.
Bid warriors build, when they burn my body,
A stately barrow on the headland's height.
It shall be for remembrance among my people
As it towers high on the Cape of the Whale,
And sailors shall know it as Beowulf's Barrow,
Sea-faring mariners driving their ships
Through fogs of ocean from far countries."
  Then the great-hearted king unclasped from his throat
A collar of gold, and gave to his thane;
Gave the young hero his gold-decked helmet,
His ring and his byrny, and wished him well:
"You are the last of the Wægmunding line.
All my kinsmen, eorls in their glory,
Fate has sent to their final doom,
And I must follow." These words were the last
The old king spoke ere the pyre received him,
The leaping flames of the funeral blaze,
And his breath went forth from his bosom, his soul
Went forth from the flesh, to the joys of the just.
  Then bitter it was for Beowulf's thane
To behold his loved one lying on earth
Suffering sore at the end of life.
The monster that slew him, the dreadful dragon,
Likewise lay broken and brought to his death.
The worm no longer could rule the hoard,

But the hard, sharp sword, the work of the hammer,
Had laid him low; and the winged dragon
Lay stretched near the barrow, broken and still.
No more in the midnight he soared in air,
Disclosing his presence, and proud of his gold;
For he sank to earth by the sword of the king.
But few of mankind, if the tales be true,
Has it prospered much, though mighty in war
And daring in deed, to encounter the breath
Of the venomous worm or plunder his wealth
When the ward of the barrow held watch o'er the mound.
Beowulf bartered his life for the treasure;
Both foes had finished this fleeting life.
Not long was it then till the laggards in battle
Came forth from the forest, ten craven in fight,
Who had dared not face the attack of the foe
In their lord's great need. The shirkers in shame
Came wearing their bucklers and trappings of war
Where the old man lay. They looked upon Wiglaf.
Weary he sat by the side of his leader
Attempting with water to waken his lord.
It availed him little; the wish was vain!
He could not stay his soul upon earth,
Nor one whit alter the will of God.
The Lord ruled over the lives of men
As He rules them still. With a stern rebuke
He reproached the cowards whose courage had failed.
Wiglaf addressed them; Weohstan's son
Gazed sad of heart on the hateful men:
"Lo! he may say who would speak the truth
That the lord who gave you these goodly rings,
This warlike armor wherein you stand—
When oft on the ale-bench he dealt to his hall-men
Helmet and byrny, endowing his thanes
With the fairest he found from near or from far—
That he grievously wasted these trappings of war
When battle befell him. The king of the folk

Had no need to boast of his friends in the fight.
But the God of victory granted him strength
To avenge himself with the edge of the sword
When he needed valor. Of little avail
The help I brought in the bitter battle!
Yet still I strove, though beyond my strength,
To aid my kinsman. And ever the weaker
The savage foe when I struck with my sword;
Ever the weaker the welling flame!
Too few defenders surrounded our ruler
When the hour of evil and terror befell.
Now granting of treasure and giving of swords,
Inherited land-right and joy of the home,
Shall cease from your kindred. And each of your clan
Shall fail of his birthright when men from afar
Hear tell of your flight and your dastardly deed.
Death is better for every eorl
Than life besmirched with the brand of shame!"...

The Funeral Pyre *

Then the son of Weohstan, stalwart in war,
Bade send command to the heads of homes
To bring from afar the wood for the burning
Where the good king lay: "Now glede shall devour,
As dark flame waxes, the warrior prince
Who has often withstood the shower of steel
When the storm of arrows, sped from the string,
Broke over shield, and shaft did service,
With feather-fittings guiding the barb."
Then the wise son of Weohstan chose from the host
Seven thanes of the king, the best of the band;
Eight heroes together they hied to the barrow
In under the roof of the fearful foe;
One of the warriors leading the way
Bore in his hand a burning brand.
They cast no lots who should loot the treasure
When they saw unguarded the gold in the hall
Lying there useless; little they scrupled
As quickly they plundered the precious store.
Over the sea-cliff into the ocean
They tumbled the dragon, the deadly worm,
Let the sea-tide swallow the guarder of gold.
Then a wagon was loaded with well-wrought treasure,
A countless number of every kind;
And the aged warrior, the white-haired king,
Was borne on high to the Cape of the Whale.
The Geat folk fashioned a peerless pyre
Hung round with helmets and battle-boards,
With gleaming byrnies as Beowulf bade.
In sorrow of soul they laid on the pyre
Their mighty leader, their well-loved lord.
The warriors kindled the bale on the barrow,

* *Beowulf* 3110–82.

Wakened the greatest of funeral fires.
Dark o'er the blaze the wood-smoke mounted;
The winds were still, and the sound of weeping
Rose with the roar of the surging flame
Till the heat of the fire had broken the body.
With hearts that were heavy they chanted their sorrow,
Singing a dirge for the death of their lord;
And an aged woman with upbound locks
Lamented for Beowulf, wailing in woe.
Over and over she uttered her dread
Of sorrow to come, of bloodshed and slaughter,
Terror of battle, and bondage and shame.
The smoke of the bale-fire rose to the sky!
The men of the Weder folk fashioned a mound
Broad and high on the brow of the cliff,
Seen from afar by seafaring men.
Ten days they worked on the warrior's barrow
Inclosing the ash of the funeral flame
With a wall as worthy as wisdom could shape.
They bore to the barrow the rings and the gems,
The wealth of the hoard the heroes had plundered.
The olden treasure they gave to the earth,
The gold to the ground, where it still remains
As useless to men as it was of yore.
Then round the mound rode the brave in battle,
The sons of warriors, twelve in a band,
Bemoaning their sorrow and mourning their king.
They sang their dirge and spoke of the hero
Vaunting his valor and venturous deeds.
So is it proper a man should praise
His friendly lord with a loving heart,
When his soul must forth from the fleeting flesh.
So the folk of the Geats, the friends of his hearth,
Bemoaned the fall of their mighty lord;
Said he was kindest of worldly kings,
Mildest, most gentle, most eager for fame.

VI

RELIGIOUS ALLEGORY

RELIGIOUS ALLEGORY

The medieval Church, to add emphasis and vividness to religious instruction, not infrequently employed allegory, and we find its shaping spirit in many Old English Christian poems. This is true of *The Whale* and *The Phoenix* of the Exeter Book. *The Whale* comprises lines 75-162 of the Old English *Physiologus*. *The Phoenix* is a complete and separate poem of 677 lines.

The legend of the Great Whale is undoubtedly of very early date. The sea-beast resembling an island, on which sailors landed and kindled a fire only to be carried down into the depths of ocean, was described in the Greek *Physiologus* as a huge sea-turtle. But in the Old English poem it is called a whale, and the description is unmistakable. In the allegorical equations of the Old English version the whale is Satan. The enticing odor that comes from the mouth of the whale is the lust of the flesh. The great jaws that close on unwary schools of fish are the gates of hell closing on the damned. The error of the sailors who mistake evil for good, and danger for safety, is the tragic error that leads to hell.

A more skillful and artistic use of allegory in Old English verse is found in *The Phoenix*, a poem which is much more than an allegorical fable. It is fashioned from a Latin poem usually attributed to Lactantius, and is one of the most graceful of the Old English religious poems. It has been claimed by some critics as the work of Cynewulf, but there is little to throw light on its authorship. The most definite conviction that comes from a study of *The Phoenix* is that its unknown author was one of the most gifted of the Old English religious poets.

The landscape of *The Phoenix* is the landscape of the Earthly Paradise. It is a tableland whose fertile soil is watered by sweet fountains, where in serene, unchanging weather no leaf withers nor fruits decay, and where nothing noisome ever intrudes. It lies near the Heavenly Paradise through whose open portals can be heard the hymns of the blessed.

At the end of every thousand years the Phoenix flies to a remote region of Syria, where in a lofty tree it builds its nest of spice-bearing twigs and fragrant herbs. There it lodges until by the sun's heat the nest kindles, and the bird is consumed. But from the ashes the Phoenix is reborn. The allegory is clearly interpreted in the poem itself. The flight of the bird from the Earthly Paradise is man's loss of Eden. The high tree in Syria is God's mercy to men. The spices and herbs of which the nest is built are the words and deeds of righteousness. In the final lines of the poem the Phoenix is explicitly equated with Christ and the Resurrection.

The Whale *

Now I will fashion the tale of a fish,
With wise wit singing in measured strains
The song of the Great Whale. Often unwittingly
Ocean-mariners meet with this monster,
Fastitocalon, fierce and menacing,
The Great Sea-Swimmer of the ocean-streams.
Like a rough rock is the Whale's appearance,
Or as if there were swaying by the shore of the sea
A great mass of sedge in the midst of the sand dunes;
So it seems to sailors they see an island,
And they firmly fasten their high-prowed ships
With anchor-ropes to the land that is no land,
Hobble their sea-steeds at ocean's end,
Land bold on the island and leave their barks
Moored at the water's edge in the wave's embrace.
There they encamp, the sea-weary sailors,
Fearing no danger. They kindle a fire;
High on the island the hot flames blaze
And joy returns to travel-worn hearts
Eager for rest. Then, crafty in evil,
When the Whale feels the sailors are fully set
And firmly lodged, enjoying fair weather,
Suddenly with his prey Ocean's Guest plunges
Down in the salt wave seeking the depths,
In the hall of death drowning sailors and ships.
Such is the manner of demons, the devils' way,
Luring from virtue, inciting to lust,
By secret power deceiving men's souls
That they may seek help at the hands of their foes
And, fixed in sin, find abode with the Fiend.
Sly and deceitful, when the Devil perceives

* *Physiologus* 75–162.

Out of hell-torment that each of mankind,
Of the race of men, is bound with his ring,
Then with cunning craft the Dark Destroyer
Takes proud and humble who here on earth
Through sin did his will. Seizing them suddenly
Shrouded in darkness, estranged from good,
He seeks out hell, the bottomless abyss
In the misty gloom; even as the Great Whale
Who drowns the mariners, sea-steeds and men.
A second trait has he, the proud Sea-Thrasher,
Even more marvelous: when hunger torments
And the fierce Water-Monster is fain of food,
Then the Ocean-Warden opens his mouth,
Unlocks his wide jaws, and a winsome odor
Comes from his belly; other kinds of fish
Are deceived thereby, all eagerly swimming
To where the sweet fragrance comes flowing forth.
In unwary schools they enter within
Till the wide mouth is filled. Then swiftly the Whale
Over his sea-prey snaps his grim jaws.
So is it with him in this transient time
Who takes heed to his life too late and too little,
Letting vain delights through their luring fragrance
Ensnare his soul till he slips away,
Soiled with sin, from the King of glory.
Before them the Devil after death's journey
Throws open hell for all who in folly
Fulfilled the lying lusts of the flesh
Against the law. But when the Wily One,
Expert in evil, has brought into bonds
In the burning heat those cleaving to him
Laden with sins, who during their life-days
Did his bidding, on them after death
His savage jaws he snaps together,
The gates of hell. Who gather there
Know no retreat, no return out thence,

31524

LIBRARY
COLLEGE OF SAN MATEO

Any more than the fishes swimming the sea
Can escape from the grip of the Great Whale.
  Therefore by every means (should every man
Serve the Lord God) and strive against devils
By words and works, that we may behold
The King of glory. In this transient time
Let us seek for peace and healing at His hands,
That we in grace may dwell with Him so dear
And have His bliss and blessedness for ever!

The Phoenix *

Lo! I have learned of the loveliest of lands
Far to the eastward, famous among men.
But few ever fare to that far-off realm
Set apart from the sinful by the power of God.
Beauteous that country and blessed with joys,
With the fairest odors of all the earth;
Goodly the island, gracious the Maker,
Matchless and mighty, who stablished the world.
There ever stand open the portals of heaven
With songs of rapture for blessed souls.
The plain is winsome, the woods are green,
Widespread under heaven. No rain or snow,
Or breath of frost or blast of fire,
Or freezing hail or fall of rime,
Or blaze of sun or bitter-long cold,
Or scorching summer or winter storm
Work harm a whit, but the plain endures
Sound and unscathed. The lovely land
Is rich with blossoms. No mountains rise,
No lofty hills, as here with us;
No high rock-cliffs, no dales or hollows,
No mountain gorges, no caves or crags,
Naught rough or rugged; but the pleasant plain
Basks under heaven laden with bloom.
Twelve cubits higher is that lovely land,
As learned writers in their books relate,
Than any of these hills that here in splendor
Tower on high under heavenly stars.
Serene that country sunny groves gleaming;
Winsome the woodlands; fruits never fail
Or shining blossoms. As God gave bidding
The groves stand for ever growing and green.

* *The Phoenix* 1–392.

Winter and summer the woods alike
Are hung with blossoms; under heaven no leaf
Withers, no fire shall waste the plain
To the end of the world. As the waters of old,
The sea-floods, covered the compass of earth
And the pleasant plain stood all uninjured,
By the grace of God unhurt and unharmed,
So shall it flourish till the fire of Judgment
When graves shall open, the dwellings of death.
Naught hostile lodges in all that land,
No pain or weeping or sign of sorrow,
No age or anguish or narrow death;
No ending of life or coming of evil,
No feud or vengeance or fret of care;
No lack of wealth or pressure of want,
No sorrow or sleeping or sore disease.
No winter storm or change of weather
Fierce under heaven, or bitter frost
With wintry icicles smites any man there.
No hail or hoar-frost descends to earth,
No windy cloud; no water falls
Driven by storm. But running streams
And welling waters wondrously spring
Overflowing earth from fountains fair.
From the midst of the wood a winsome water
Each month breaks out from the turf of earth,
Cold as the sea-stream, coursing sweetly
Through all the grove. By the bidding of God
The flood streams forth through the glorious land
Twelve times yearly. The trees are hung
With beauteous increase, flowering buds;
Holy under heaven the woodland treasures
Wane not nor wither; no failing bloom,
No fruits of the wildwood, fall to earth;
But in every season on all the trees
The boughs bear their burden of fruit anew.
Green are the groves in the grassy meadow,

Gaily garnished by the might of God.
No branch is broken, and fragrance fair
Fills all the land. Nor ever comes change
Till the Ruler Whose wisdom wrought its beginning
His ancient Creation shall bring to its end.
In that woodland dwelleth, most wondrous fair
And strong of wing, a fowl called Phoenix;
There dauntless-hearted he has his home,
His lonely lodging. In that lovely land
Death shall never do him a hurt,
Or work him harm while the world standeth.
Each day he observes the sun's bright journey
Greeting God's candle, the gleaming gem,
Eagerly watching till over the ocean
The fairest of orbs shines forth from the East,
God's bright token glowing in splendor,
The ancient hand-work of the Father of all.
The stars are hid in the western wave,
Dimmed at dawn, and the dusky night
Steals darkly away; then, strong of wing
And proud of pinion, the bird looks out
Over the ocean under the sky,
Eagerly waiting when up from the East
Heaven's gleam comes gliding over the wide water.
Then the fair bird, changeless in beauty,
Frequents at the fountain the welling streams;
Twelve times the blessed one bathes in the burn
Ere the bright beacon comes, the candle of heaven;
And even as often at every bath
Tastes the pleasant water of brimcold wells.
Thereafter the proud one after his water-play
Takes his flight to a lofty tree
Whence most easily o'er the eastern ways
He beholds the course of the heavenly taper
Brightly shining over the tossing sea,
A blaze of light. The land is made beautiful,
The world made fair, when the famous gem

O'er the ocean-stretches illumines the earth
All the world over, noblest of orbs.
When the sun climbs high over the salt streams
The gray bird wings from his woodland tree
And, swift of pinion, soars to the sky
Singing and caroling to meet the sun.
Then is the bearing of the bird so fair,
Its heart so gladsome and so graced with joy,
It trills its song in clear-voiced strain,
More wondrous music than ever child of man
Heard under heaven since the High-King,
Author of glory, created the world,
The earth and the heavens. The music of its hymn
Is sweeter than all song-craft, more winsome and fair
Than any harmony. Neither trumpet nor horn,
Nor melody of harp is like to that lay,
Nor voice of man, nor strain of organ music,
Nor swan's singing feathers, nor any pleasant sound
That God gave for joy to men in this mournful world.
So he hymns and carols with joyous heart
Until the sun in the southern sky
Sinks to its setting. Then in silence he listens;
Thrice the wise-hearted lifts his head,
Thrice shakes his feathers strong in flight,
Then broods in silence. Twelve times the bird
Notes the hours of night and day.
So is it ordained for the forest dweller
To live in that land having joy of life,
Well-being and bliss and all the world's beauty,
Till the warden of the wood of this life's winters
Has numbered a thousand. Aged and old
The gray-plumed is weary and weighted with years.
Then the fairest of fowls flies from the greenwood,
The blossoming earth, seeks a boundless realm,
A land and lodging where no man dwells;
And there exalted over all the host
Has dominion and rule of the race of birds,

With them in the waste resides for a season.
Swift of pinion and strong in flight
He wings to the westward, heavy with years.
Around the royal one throng the birds,
Servants and thanes of a peerless prince.
And so he seeks out the Syrian land
With a lordly following. There the pure fowl
Suddenly leaves them, lodging in shadow
In a woodland covert, a secret spot
Sequestered and hidden from the hosts of men.
  There he takes lodging in a lofty tree
Fast by its roots in the forest-wood
Under heaven's roof. The race of men
Call the tree Phoenix from the name of the fowl.
Unto that tree, as I have heard tell,
The Great King has granted, the Lord of mankind,
That it alone of all tall trees
Is the brightest blooming in all the earth.
Nor may aught of evil work it a harm;
For ever shielded, for ever unscathed,
It stands to the end while the world standeth.
  When the wind lies at rest and weather is fair,
And heaven's bright gem shines holy on high,
When clouds are dispersed and seas are tranquil
And every storm is stilled under heaven,
When the weather-candle shines warm from the south
Lighting earth's legions, then in the boughs
He begins to form and fashion a nest.
His sage heart stirs with a great desire
Swiftly to alter old age to youth,
To renew his life. From near and far
He gleans and gathers to his lodging-place
Pleasant plants and fruits of the forest,
All sweetest spices and fragrant herbs
Which the King of glory, Lord of beginnings,
Created on earth for a blessing to men,
The sweetest under heaven. So he assembles

In the boughs of the tree his shining treasures.
There in that waste-land the wild bird
In the tall tree's top timbers his house
Pleasant and lovely. And there he lodges
In that lofty chamber; in the leafy shade
Besets his feathered body on every side
With the sweetest odors and blossoms of earth.
When the gem of the sky in the summer season,
The burning sun, shines over the shades
Scanning the world, the Phoenix sits
Fain of departure, fulfilling his fate.
His house is kindled by heat of the sun;
The herbs grow hot, the pleasant hall steams
With sweetest odors; in the surging flame,
In the fire-grip, burns the bird with his nest.
The pyre is kindled, the fire enfolds
The home of the heart-sick. The yellow flame
Fiercely rages; the Phoenix burns,
Full of years, as the fire consumes
The fleeting body. The spirit fades,
The soul of the fated. The bale-fire seizes
Both bone and flesh.
But his life is reborn
After a season, when the ashes begin
After the fire-surge fusing together
Compressed to a ball. The brightest of nests,
The house of the stout-heart, by force of the flame
Is clean consumed; the corpse grows chill;
The bone-frame is broken; the burning subsides.
From the flame of the fire is found thereafter
In the ash of the pyre an apple's likeness,
Of which grows a worm most wondrous fair,
As it were a creature come from an egg,
Shining from the shell. In the shadow it grows
Fashioned first as an eagle's young,
A comely fledgling; then flourishing fair
Is like in form to a full-grown eagle

Adorned with feathers as he was at first,
Brightly gleaming.
Then is beauty reborn,
Sundered from sin, once more made new;
Even in such fashion as men, for food,
Bring home in harvest at reaping time
Pleasant fare, the fruits of earth,
Ere coming of winter lest rain-storms waste;
Find joy and strength in their garnered store
When frost and snow with furious might
Cover earth over with winter weeds:
From these grains again grow riches for men
Through the sprouting kernels, first sowed pure seed
Then the warm sun in Spring-time, symbol of life,
Wakes the world's wealth and new crops rise,
Each after its kind, the treasures of earth.
Even so the Phoenix after long life
Grows young and fashioned with flesh anew.
He eats no food, no fare of earth,
But only a drop of honey-dew
Which falls in the midnight; thereby the Phoenix
Comforts his life till he comes again
To his own habitation, his ancient seat.
Beset with his sweet herbs, proud of plumage,
The bird is reborn, his life made young,
Youthful and gifted with every grace.
Then from the ground he gathers together
The nimble body that the bale-fire broke;
With skill assembles the ashy remnants,
The crumbling bones left after the blaze;
Brings together there bone and ashes
And covers over with savory herbs
The spoil of the death-fire, fairly adorned.
Then he takes his departure, turns to his home,
Grasps in his talons, clasps in his claws,
What the fire has left; joyously flying
To his native dwelling, his sun-bright seat,

His happy homeland. All is renewed,
Life and feathered body as it was at first
What time God placed him in that pleasant plain.
He brings there the bones which the fiery surges
Swallowed in flame on the funeral pyre,
The ashes as well; and all together
Buries the leavings, ashes and bone,
In his island home. For him is renewed
The sign of the sun when the light of heaven,
Brightest of orbs, most joyous of jewels,
Over the ocean shines from the East.
Fair-breasted that fowl and comely of hue
With varied colors; the head behind
Is emerald burnished and blended with scarlet.
The tail plumes are colored some crimson, some brown,
And cunningly speckled with shining spots.
White of hue are the backs of the wings,
The neck all green beneath and above.
The strong neb gleams like glass or gem;
Without and within the beak is fair.
The eye is stark, most like to stone
Or shining jewel skillfully wrought
In a golden setting by cunning smiths.
All round the neck like the ring of the sun
Is a shining circlet fashioned of feathers.
Wondrously bright and shining the belly,
Brilliant and comely; over the back
Splendidly fashioned the shield is spread.
The fair bird's shanks, its yellow feet
Are patterned with scales. 'Tis a peerless fowl
Most like in appearance to a peacock proud,
As the writings say; neither sluggish or slow,
Torpid or slothful, as some birds are
Heavily winging their way in the sky;
But swift and lively and very light,
Fair and goodly and marked with glory.
Eternal the God who grants him that grace!

Then from that country the Phoenix flies
To seek his homeland, his ancient seat.
He wings his way observed of men
Assembled together from south and north,
From East and west, in hurrying hosts.
A great folk gathers from far and near
To behold God's grace in the beauteous bird
For whom at Creation the Lord of all
Ordained and stablished a special nature,
A fairer perfection beyond all fowl.
Men on earth all marvel in wonder
At the fair fowl's beauty inscribing in books
And skillfully carving on marble stone
When the day and the hour shall exhibit to men
The gleaming beauty of the flying bird.
Then all about him the race of birds
In flocks assemble on every side,
Winging from far ways, singing his praises,
Hymning their hero in fervent strains;
Around the Phoenix in circling flight
They attend the holy one high in air,
Thronging in multitudes. Men look up,
Marvel to see that happy host
Worship the wild bird, flock after flock,
Keenly acclaiming and praising as King
Their beloved lord; joyously leading
Their liege to his home; till at last alone
He swiftly soars where that blissful band
May not follow after when the best of birds
From the turf of earth returns to his homeland.
So the blessed bird after his death-bale
Enters once more his ancient abode,
His fatherland fair. Leaving their leader
The birds sad-hearted return to their home,
Their prince to his palace. God only knows,
The Almighty King, what his breed may be,
Or male or female; and no man knows,

But only the Maker, the ancient edict
And wondrous causes of that fowl's kind.
There blessed abiding the bird has bliss
In the welling streams and the woodland grove
Till a thousand winters have waxed and waned,
And again life ends as the bale-fire burns,
The ravaging flames; yet he rises again,
Strangely, wondrously wakened to life.
Therefore drooping he dreads not death,
Dire death-pangs, but ever he knows
After the fire's force life refashioned,
Breath after burning, and straight transformed
Out of the ashes, once more restored
Unto bird's form his youth is reborn
Under sheltering skies. He is himself
Both his own son and his own dear father;
Ever the heir of his former remains.
The Almighty Maker of all mankind
Has granted him wondrously once more to be
What before he was, with feathers appareled
Though fire clasp him close in its grip.
So each blessed soul through somber death
After his life-days of sore distress
Gains life everlasting, knowing God's grace
In bliss never-ending; and ever thereafter
Resides in glory as reward for his works.
The traits of this bird clearly betoken
Christ's chosen thanes, how on earth they thrill
By the Father's grace with a gleaming joy
In this perilous time, and attain thereafter
Bliss on high in the heavenly home.

VII

OLD TESTAMENT AND APOCRYPHAL VERSE

OLD TESTAMENT AND APOCRYPHAL VERSE

The poetic narrative of Lucifer's rebellion and the Fall of Man is found in the Old English *Genesis*, the first poem of the Junius MS. *Genesis* consists of two parts: section *A*, lines 1-234 and 852 to the end; and section *B*, lines 235-851. Section *B* is an interpolation into a break in section *A* and is, in part at least, a transcription from an Old Saxon poem. The opening lines of *Genesis* deal with the rebellion of Lucifer, and this material is supplemented in *Christ and Satan*, of the same MS, by a series of "lamentations" of the fallen angels. After rehearsing the rebellion and fall of Lucifer, *Genesis* goes on to recount the story of Creation and the Fall of Man.

In *Genesis B* and *Christ and Satan*, both source material and its poetic shaping go far beyond Biblical paraphrase. In both poems we find dramatic versification of material gathered from many sources and blended into what became known as the Hexaemeral tradition. The stream of this tradition included commentaries on the Hexaemeron, or six days of the Creation as recorded in the Biblical Genesis, and the exegetical writings of the Church Fathers.

A series of Lenten sermons by Bishop Basil of Caesarea was an early work specifically devoted to discussion of the Creation. Against a Scriptural background, there came to be associated with the story of Creation accounts of the Revolt of the Angels and the Fall of Man. The inclusion of these three themes in poetic form in the Junius MS takes on the nature of an unformed cosmic trilogy. In the volume and scope of the Hexaemeral tradition we find apocryphal legend like the *Vita* of Adam and Eve; patristic commentary such as Bede's *Commentary on Genesis*, an Old English *Hexaemeron* often attributed to Ælfric; and similar writings of Churchmen and scholars.

The temptation scene in *Genesis B* varies in important respects from the Biblical account. The Tempter appears to Adam and Eve disguised as an angelic messenger claiming that God has sent him to revoke the ban on the forbidden fruit. Rejected by Adam he turns to Eve, who is convinced and eats of the fruit. She joins in persuading Adam to eat, saying she knows by the messenger's raiment that he comes from God, and that Adam is refusing obedience to God's new command. All this she does, the poet tells us, with a loyal heart. The assumption of angelic form by agents of evil is, of course, not unique in *Genesis B*. It is a device of deception employed in the apocryphal *Vita* of Adam and Eve, and found in many legends of the saints, among them Cynewulf's poem based on a Latin life of St. Juliana of Nicomedia.

Lamentations of the Fallen Angels *

There out of hell the Old One bellows
With bitter outcry and baleful voice
Bewailing his woe: "Whither is fled
The wealth of bliss we should have in heaven?
This is the home of darkness dreadfully bound
With fettering bonds of fire. The floor of hell
Is a blaze of flame burning with poison.
Not far is the end when we all together
Must suffer torment, torture and pain,
No longer possessing the splendor of glory
In heaven above, or joy in her high halls.
"Lo! once of old before the face of God
In happier hours we knew heavenly bliss
Singing in glory, where now round Eternal God
The righteous dwell in heaven's high hall
Adoring the Lord with words and works,
While I in this torment must abide in bonds,
Nor hope for a better home, because of my pride. . . .
"I was a holy angel in heaven of old
Dear unto God; knew delight with the Lord,
Great joy with our Maker; this multitude likewise.
But I planned in my heart to hurl from His throne
The Splendor of glory, the Son of God;
To rule over all things with this wretched band
Which I have brought home to hell. Clear was the token
When I was cast down to perdition, deep under earth
To the bottomless pit. I have brought you all
From your native home to a house of bondage.
"Here is no glory of wealth, no wine-hall of the proud,
No worldly joys or angelic, no hope of heaven.
This foul home flames with fire. I am God's foe!
Ever at the doors of hell dragons stand guard

* *Christ and Satan* 34–50; 81–105; 129–77.

Fierce and flaming. Hope not for help from them!
This terrible home is filled full with horror.
We have nowhere to hide our heads in the gloom of hell,
Or cover ourselves in the depths with shadows of darkness.
Here is the adder's hiss! Here serpents dwell!
Firmly the bonds of pain are fastened upon us.
Fierce are the fiends of hell, dusky and dark.
Day never lightens this gloom nor the glory of God....
"I am so large of limb I may not lie hid
In this wide hall, wounded with my sins.
At times cold and heat in hell are mingled;
At times I can hear the hell-slaves howl,
A wretched race bewailing this realm of pain
Deep under the nesses where naked men
Struggle with serpents. All this windy hall
Is filled with horror. Never shall I know
A happier home, city or stronghold,
Nor ever mine eyes have sight of the gleaming world again.
"Worse is it now for me that ever I knew
The gleaming light of glory with angels on high,
And the harmonies of heaven where hosts of the blessed
Encircle the Son of God with sweetest song.
No evil can I bring on any soul
Except those only whom God casts out.
These I may have in thrall in the bondage of hell,
Bring to their long abode in the bitter abyss.
"How unlike are we all to those earlier days
When once we had beauty in heaven, honor and bliss.
Often the sons of God sang hymns of glory
When as thanes about our Beloved we praised the Lord,
Sang glory to God. But now I am stained with my sins,
Branded with evil; now burning with fire
I must bear on my back the bondage of torment,
Hot in hell, without hope of good."
And still the Foul Fiend, shepherd of sins,
Cried out of hell in torment accursed.
The words he spoke flew forth in sparks,

Most like to poison as he poured them out:
"Farewell to the glory of God! Farewell to the Helm of hosts!
Farewell to the might of the Maker. Farewell to the world!
Farewell to the light of day and the grace of God!
Farewell to the angel host! Farewell to heaven!
Alas! that I have lost those lasting joys!
Alas! that I may not reach with my hands to heaven above,
Nor thither lift up mine eyes, nor hear with my ears
The pealing trumpet sound, because from His seat
I would have driven God's Son and seized for myself
Dominion of glory and grace. Worse fate befell
Than I could foresee. From the shining host I am severed,
Cast down from light into this loathsome home."

The Temptation and Fall of Man *

With mighty hand the Holy Lord,
All-Ruling God, had stablished and strengthened
Ten angel orders in whom He trusted
That they would serve Him and work His will,
Since the Holy Lord with His hands had shaped them,
Had given them reason and granted them bliss.
He made one so strong, so mighty of mind;
Gave him such power next unto God
In the heavenly kingdom; shaped him so shining;
So fair the form God fashioned for him;
That his beauty was like to the blazing stars.
He should have said praises and prayers unto God,
Prizing his bliss and blessing in heaven;
Should have thanked his Lord for His gifts in light
Which God would have let him long enjoy.
But he turned it all to a terrible outcome;
Began to stir up strife against God,
Heaven's Highest Ruler on His holy throne. . . .
"Why must I slave? What need (quoth he)
That I serve a master? My hands have might
To work many wonders. I have strength to rear
A goodlier throne, a higher in heaven.
Why must I yield or fawn for His favor
Or bow in submission? I may be God
As well as He. Brave comrades stand by me,
Stout-hearted heroes unfailing in strife.
These fighters fierce have made me their leader;
With such may one plan and muster support.
They are loyal friends and faithful of heart;
I may be their lord and rule this realm.
So it seems not good that I grovel before God
For any boon. I will obey Him no longer."

* *Genesis* 246–60; 278–300; 347–88; 408–730; 751–62.

Now when the Almighty had heard these words,
How the arrogant angel was rousing revolt
From his Lord and Leader in insolent folly,
Needs must he pay for that deed of pride,
Know the pain of that struggle, and suffer his punishment,
Most dreadful of deaths. So every man shall,
Whoever wickedly wars against God,
The Lord of might! Heaven's Ruler was roused
And hurled him in wrath from his heavenly throne. . . .
Then spoke Satan in sorrow of spirit,
Who must henceforth rule o'er the depths of hell.
Once he was white, God's angel in heaven,
Till his heart betrayed him, his haughty pride,
And he would not obey or honor the word
Of the Lord of hosts. Hell's heat was around him,
His heart surged within him; he spoke these words:
"Unlike indeed is this narrow land
To that other home that of old we held
In heaven's high realm, though we could not keep
What our Lord had granted, or govern our kingdom
Against God's will. He has wrought us wrong,
In hurling us down to the fiery depths of hell,
Deprived of heaven. He has marked those heights
For man to settle. 'Tis my greatest sorrow
That Adam, fashioned and formed of earth,
Should hold my high seat and abide in bliss
While we suffer this torture, this torment in hell.
"Woe! Alas! Could I lift my hands
And feel their strength, be free for an hour,
One winter hour, with this host I would—
But bands of iron bind me about,
Sorely the rings of my bondage ride me!
I am stripped of my kingdom. Firmly hell's fetters
Are fastened upon me; the fires burn
Above and below. A loathlier landscape
I never have seen, flame unassuaged
Surging through hell. These clasping shackles,

These cruel-hard chains, hinder my going.
Hell's doors are bolted, the ways are barred,
My hands are fastened, my feet are bound,
I can no way get free of these fettering chains.
Gratings huge of heavy iron,
Hammered hot, press hard upon me,
Wherewith God has fastened me firm by the neck.
I know full well that He knew my purpose
Of evil for Adam and all his hopes
Of the heavenly realm, had I power of my hands. . . .
"Begin now to plan and plot this assault!
If to any thane ever in days of old
When we dwelt in that good kingdom and happily held our thrones
I dealt out princely treasure, at no dearer time
Could he give me requital, repayment for gifts,
If some thane would be my helper and outward hence
Break through these bolted gates, with strength to wing
On feathered pinions circling in the sky
To where new-shaped on earth Adam and Eve
Abide in bliss surrounded with abundance,
While we are cast out hither to this deep hell.
"They now indeed are dearer unto God
And have the wealth that we should have in heaven,
Our rightful realm. The advantage lies with man!
My soul is sorrowful, my heart is sore
That they should hold the heavenly realms for ever.
If one of you can win them in any way
To forsake God's law, they will lose His love;
If they break His commandment His mood will be roused
And all their wealth will be changed for the worse,
Their punishment made ready, some penalty grim.
Take thought how you may ensnare them. More softly then
Shall I lie in these chains if they lose the heavenly kingdom.
Whoever shall bring that to pass shall have portion for ever
In all we may win of advantage in these wide flames.
I will let him sit next myself who returns to tell,
In this hot hell, that the will of the King of heaven

Unworthily they forswore by their words and works."...[1]
Then God's enemy began to arm,
To put on his war-gear. He had a wily heart.
He placed on his head the helmet of darkness,
Fastened the buckles and bound it firm.
He had craft of speech and cunning of word.
He circled upward and darted out
Through the portals of hell. (He had a pitiless heart.)
Fell of purpose he soared in flight
Cleaving the fire with fiendish craft.
He wished to ensnare God's servants in sin,
Seduce and beguile them until they had gained God's hate.
With fiendish cunning he found his way
To where on earth he came upon Adam,
God's own handiwork wisely fashioned
And Eve beside him, fairest of women,
Serving God well in all good works
For the Maker of man had made them His stewards.
By them two trees stood filled with fruit
And clothed with increase. Heaven's High King,
The Almighty, had set them that the sons of men
Might choose of good or evil, weal or woe.
Unlike was their fruit. One tree was fair,
Lovely and shining, pleasant and sweet.
That was the tree of life! He might live for ever,
Who ate of that fruit. Nor would age thereafter
Or woeful sickness work him a hurt;
But long might he live in happiness for ever,
Have here on earth the favor of heaven's King
And the glory ordained on high when he went hence.
The other tree was in shadow, sunless and dark;
That was the tree of death! Deadly its fruit!

[1] At this point in the MS a leaf or two is missing. The lost text must have dealt in some detail with the response to this *comitatus* appeal of the chained and shackled Satan. Evidently one of his followers came forward and was accepted as his agent in evil. As the text continues after the break, this deputy of Satan is pictured as "God's enemy" arming himself for the work of revenge.

Disgraced in this world, knowing good and evil,
He needs must suffer in sorrow and sweat
Who ate of the fruit that formed on that tree.
Old age would despoil him of deeds of strength,
Of bliss and lordship, with death for his lot.
A little time only he might joy in this life,
Then seek in the flames the most loathsome of lands,
Be subject to fiends where most fearful horrors
Afflict men for ever. That the fiend knew well,
The devil's dark steward who strove against God.
Then the fiend put on the form of the serpent
In twining coils round the tree of death;
Took of the fruit and turned him thence
To where he saw Adam, God's handiwork.
With wily falsehood from the first word
The devil began to ask of Adam:
"Have you any longing, Adam, that looks to God?
I come in His service, faring from afar;
Nor has time been long since I sat at His side.
On this errand He sent me, bade you eat of this fruit;
Said your power and might and your mind will be greater,
Your body brighter, your form more fair,
And you shall lack naught of the world's wealth.
Because you have done His will and won His favor,
And served Him with gladness, you are dear unto God.
In His heavenly light I have heard Him speak
Of your way of life, praising your words and works.
"So must you also obey the bidding
His heralds bring you hither to this land.
Wide reaching are the green realms of the world
And God, the All-Ruler, reigns in the highest heavens.
He does not wish to have the hardship
Of making this journey but sends His servants
To tell His commandments, bidding us teach
Wisdom by precept. Now do His will,
Take this fruit in your hand, taste it and eat.
Your heart will grow roomy, your form more fair.

The Lord, your God, sent this help from heaven."
Then Adam answered where he stood on earth,
The first of men: "When I heard the Almighty,
The Victor Lord speaking with solemn voice,
And He bade me dwell here and do His will,
Gave me the woman, this glowing bride,
And bade me guard that I be not beguiled
Or ever tempted to the tree of death,
He said that blackest hell shall hold him fast
Who harbors in his heart one whit of evil.
Though you come with lies and with cunning guile
I do not know that you come from God,
An angel from heaven. I can understand nothing
Of the bidding you bring, of your errand or sayings,
Of your words or ways. But well I know
What our Saviour said when last I saw Him:
To honor His word and keep it well,
To fulfill His law. You are not like
Any of His angels that ever I saw,
Nor do I find in you any token of faith
That God has sent me as sign of His favor.
Therefore I can not hearken. Get you hence!
I fix my faith on Almighty God
Whose hands created me. From His high kingdom
He can give us all good things, though He send no servant."
Then the tempter in anger turned unto Eve
Where he saw her standing, the lovely woman.
He said that thereafter her offspring would suffer
The worst of all evils: "I know well that God
Will be much displeased with the message I bring,
When I come from my weary journey over this long way
To tell Him you will not heed the new behest
He sends you out of the East. He only, forsooth,
Must come to instruct you; His messengers may not
Tell you His bidding! Truly I know
The Almighty's wrath will be roused against you.
"But if willingly, O woman, you hear my words

Your mind will be freer, your wit more firm
To ponder good counsel. Plan in your heart
That you both may avert the vengeance to come,
As I shall show you. Eat of this fruit!
Then your eyes shall have light to look afar
Over all the world, even unto the throne
Of your Lord in heaven, and have His favor.
Over Adam thereafter you shall have sway
If you have the will and he trusts your words.
If you tell him truly the precepts you heed
To work God's will and keep His commandments,
He will cease this strife, these evil answers,
As we both shall urge him to his own good.
Entreat him earnestly to follow your teaching
Lest you grow displeasing to the Lord, your God.
"If you can perfect this attempt, O fairest of women,
I will conceal from your Lord Adam's insolent speech,
His churlish words. He charges me with falsehood,
Says I am eager in evil, no angel of God
But a servant of fiends! Yet I know full well
All the angel orders and heaven's high span,
So long was the time I served my Lord
With loyal heart. I am not like a devil."
And so with lies and with luring wiles
He urged the woman to that deed of evil,
Till the serpent's words began to work within her
(For God had fashioned for her a feebler mind),
And her heart inclined according to his counsel.
Defying God's bidding she took from the fiend
The fatal fruit of the tree of death.
Never was worse deed ordained for men!
Great is the wonder that Eternal God
Would ever permit so many of His servants
To be tricked with lies that came as good counsel.
She ate of the apple and set at naught
The word and the will of Almighty God.
Then she saw afar by gift of the fiend

Who misled her with lies and shrewdly deceived her
So that earth and heaven and all this world,
The mighty and wondrous work of God,
Seemed to her fairer and filled with light.
She beheld it not by human vision
But the devil slyly deceived her soul
And gave her sight to see afar
O'er the heavenly kingdom. With hostile heart
The cursed one spake: (No boon was his counsel!)
"O worthy Eve! You may see for yourself
How you now have altered, nor need I tell
How bright your beauty or your form how fair,
Since you trusted my words and followed my teaching.
All round about you shines radiant light
Which I brought from God, blazing from heaven.
Lo! You may touch it! Tell Adam in truth
What vision you have, what virtue, through my coming.
Even yet, if humbly he will hear my words
I will give him abundance of this good light
Wherewith I have blessed you. Nor will I upbraid
Or charge against him his graceless speech
Though he does not deserve to have it condoned,
So great the ill will he uttered against me."
So must their offspring live thereafter:
When they do evil they must earn God's grace,
Make amends to God for their grievous wrong
And have His help and eternal favor.
Then went unto Adam the fairest of women,
The winsomest maid that ever came into this world,
For she was the handiwork of the King of heaven,
Though so slyly ensnared and misled with lies
That through fiendish craft and the devil's cunning
She grew hateful to God, forfeited His favor,
And lost her glory and her heavenly home
For many a while. Woe to the man
Who departs not from evil when he has the power!
Some she bore in her hands, some on her breast,

Of the fatal apples, the fruit of the tree
Which God forbade her, the Giver of glory,
Saying His servants need not suffer death.
Holy God gave all men a heavenly home
And abundant blessings if they would but forgo
The fearful harvest, the bitter fruit,
Which that baleful tree bore on its branches.
Those were the boughs of death which the Lord forbade!
But the loathed of the Lord, the tempter, betrayed her
Into God's hatred, misled with lies;
Deceived Eve's soul, the woman's weak will,
Till she trusted his words and followed his teaching.
She believed that his counsel came from God
As he cunningly said and showed her a token,
A pledge of good faith and of friendly heart.
Then she said to her liege:
"Adam, my lord,
This fruit is so sweet and blithe in the breast;
This shining envoy is God's good angel;
I see by his garb he is sent by our Lord,
The Warden of heaven. Better that we
Should win his favor than have his ill will;
If today you made answer with aught of evil
He will still forgive if we do his service.
Of what avail is this venomous strife
With the angel of God? We need his good will.
He can plead our cause with the Almighty Prince,
The King of heaven. I can see from here
Where He sits in splendor in the South and East,
Who shaped this world. I can see His angels
Wheeling about Him in winged flight,
Unnumbered legions, most lovely of hosts.
Who could bestow such virtue and vision
Unless it came from the heavenly King?
"Far can I hear, far can I see
Through all the world and the wide Creation;
I can hear the hymns of rapture in heaven.

My heart is illumined from without and within
Since I ate of the apple. Here in my hands
I bring this fruit and give of it freely.
O good my lord, I do believe
It is come from God and brought by His bidding,
As in truthful words this herald has told me.
It is like naught else in all the earth
Except, as he says, it is sent by God."
  Over and over she urged him, all the long day
Driving Adam to that dark deed,
That they disobey the bidding of God.
The fiend stood near inflaming desire,
Boldly enticed him, cunningly tempted.
Full close stood the fiend who came from afar
On that fatal mission. He planned that men
Should be driven down unto utter death,
Deceived and misled so that they would lose
The Almighty's gift, the grace of God
And their heavenly home. The hell-fiend knew
They must bear God's wrath and bitter affliction,
Sore bondage in hell, because they forsook
The will of God when with lying words
He misled to that folly the lovely maid,
The fairest of women, till she spoke as he willed
And helped to seduce the work of God's hand.
  Over and over the most winsome of women
Pled with Adam until Adam's mind
Began to change, and he trusted the token
The woman offered. Yet she did it all
With a loyal heart and knew not the harm,
The fearful afflictions that would follow for men,
When she hearkened to the counsel of the hateful herald.
She thought by her words to win God's favor
When she offered Adam that token of truth
And the heart of the man was moved in his breast,
And his soul was turned unto Eve's desire.
  From the woman's hand he took death and hell,

Though it bore not these names but the name of fruit.
Yet the sleep of death and the devil's seduction,
Death and damnation, perdition of men,
Were the fatal fruit whereon they had feasted.
When the apple within him touched at his heart,
Then laughed aloud the fierce-hearted fiend,
Capered about, thanked his lord for both:
  "Now have I won your favor and done your will.
For many a day is man undone,
Adam and Eve. They shall know God's anger
Because they neglected His word and His will. . . .
  "Blithe may your heart be in your breast!
For here today are two things done:
The sons of men shall lose their heavenly mansions
And come to your kingdom to the fiery flames;
Also, heart-sorrow and grief are ordained for God.
Whatsoever of evil we suffer here
Is now repaid to Adam in the anger of God,
In man's perdition and the pangs of death.
Therefore my mind is healed, my heart made roomy,
For all our harms are avenged, and the hurt we suffered.
Now I return to the flames and seek out Satan
Where he lies in the darkness of hell loaded with chains."

VIII

CYNEWULF AND HIS FOLLOWERS

CYNEWULF AND HIS FOLLOWERS

With the evidence available, no poetry can be definitely attributed to Cynewulf beyond the four poems that bear his signature in runic letters, woven into the text near the end of each poem. These are the *Juliana*, *Elene*, *Ascension*, and *Fates of the Apostles*. Cynewulf's motive for his signatures was not pride of authorship or desire for fame. It was the wish of a deeply religious poet for the prayers of his readers. This he explicitly states in *Juliana*, lines 718–22: "I ask each man who may recite this poem to remember me by my name (*bi noman minum*), and pray that God may be merciful to me in the Great Day." The same motive for signature is stated in the *Fates of the Apostles*.

Of Cynewulf's signed poems two, the *Juliana* and *Elene*, are poetic narratives based on saints' legends. The legend of Juliana (*Acta Sanctorum* for February 16) tells the story of the martyrdom of St. Juliana of Nicomedia. The poem for which Cynewulf uses this material has every sign of being an early work. The *Elene* (*Acta Sanctorum* for May 4) retells in detail the Finding of the Cross by Helena, mother of the Roman Emperor Constantine. Constantine's vision of the Cross, his battle with the Huns, and Helena's embarkation and sea-voyage are vividly pictured. The *Ascension* closely parallels a Latin homily on the Ascension by Gregory. The *Fates of the Apostles* is a versified martyrology.

Other fine religious poems seem to show Cynewulfian influence, but there is no evidence as to their authorship. One of these is the *Dream of the Rood*. Set in the frame of the medieval dream-vision, it is one of the loveliest of all the Old English religious poems. It expresses with lyric grace an adoration that finds its symbol in the Cross. Because of its style, and an intimate personal reference similar to the personal passages in the signed poems, some scholars have been inclined to regard the *Dream* as the work of Cynewulf.

The *Advent Lyrics* are poetic elaborations of antiphons appointed to be sung in the services of the medieval Church at Lauds, Vespers, and other Hours during the Advent season. The antiphons on which they are based are variously interpretative of the significance of the Coming of Christ. The most characteristic feature of these lyrics is the blending of the poet's gift and the Churchman's concern with the doctrinal mysteries of the Advent.

The Last Judgment reflects a variety of sources. Its structural design is governed by the alphabetic hymn, *Apparebit repentina dies magna Domini*, quoted by Bede in the *De Arte Metrica*. Many passages of the poem are reflections of writings of Gregory, Augustine, Caesarius of Arles, and others. The entire poem has sustained creative energy in a cosmic panorama that begins with the sounding trumpets of Doomsday, and ends with the light of the Cross shining over all Creation, in place of the sun.

Constantine's Vision of the Cross *

The year was the sixth of Constantine's sway
Since he was raised up in the Roman kingdom
To be battle-lord and leader in war.
He was eager for praise, defender of peoples,
Unto men merciful; his princely might
Increased under heaven. He was true king,
War-lord of peoples. God prospered him
In glory and might so that for many
Through all the earth he became a comfort,
Defending the folk, when against the foe
He took up weapons.
He was threatened with war,
Tumult of battle. The Hunnish tribe
And the Hreth-Goths also assembled a host.
Fierce in strife marched the Franks and the Hugas;
Bold men were they and ready for battle.
War-spears glittered and woven mail;
With shout and shield they raised their standards.
The men of war were openly mustered,
The clan was gathered, the folk fared forth.
The wolf in the wood sang his song of war,
Hid not his hope of carnage to come.
The wet-winged eagle clamored and cried
As he followed the foe. Straight through the cities
The greatest of battle-hosts hasted to war
In hordes as many as the Hunnish king
Might anywhere muster of neighboring men,
Mail-clad warriors. The mightiest of armies
Went forth to battle in bands made strong
With mounted legions, till in foreign land
They boldly camped on the Danube's bank
Near the river's torrent with tumult of men.

* Cynewulf's *Elene* 7–147.

Fain would they conquer the kingdom of Rome,
Plunder and waste it. The approach of the Huns
Was known through the cities. And Caesar bade
Against the fierce foe's flying arrows
Summon the warriors straightway to strife,
Bring men to battle under the sky.
Straightway the Romans, strong in might,
Were weaponed for battle though their war-band was less
Than rode round the ruthless king of the Huns.
Then shields resounded and war-wood sang;
The king with his troops advanced to attack.
The raven clamored cruel and dark.
The host moved forward; horn-bearers leaped;
Heralds shouted; horses trod earth;
The army assembled, the stalwart to strife.
Then the king was affrighted, shaken with fear,
When he beheld the foreign foe,
The army of Huns, the horde of the Hreth-Goths,
Who there at the Roman Empire's end
On the river's margin mustered their host,
A countless force. The Roman king
Endured heart-sorrow. No hope had he
Of winning the battle for want of strength.
He had too few warriors, trusted comrades,
Against that overmight of stalwart men.
There the army encamped, eorls round their prince,
Near to the river for the night-long time
After first they beheld the march of the foe.
Then to great Caesar as he lay in slumber
Asleep with his train was a vision revealed.
To him appeared a beauteous Presence,
In man's shape made manifest,
White and shining, more fair of form
Than early or late he beheld under heaven.
He started from slumber, did on his boar-helm,
And straightway the herald, fair heavenly form,
Spoke unto Caesar, named him by name,

And the veil of darkness vanished away:
"O Constantine, the King of angels,
Leader of nations and Lord of fate,
Proclaims a compact. Be not afraid
Though these foreign tribes threaten with terror,
With hard battle. To heaven look up,
To the Prince of glory. There find support
And a token of triumph."
Straightway the king
Opened his heart to the angel's bidding
And looked on high as the herald bade,
Fair weaver of concord. Clothed with treasure
O'er the roof of clouds he beheld the Cross
Adorned with gold; its jewels glittered.
The radiant Tree was written round
With gleaming letters of glowing light:
"With this sign thou shalt halt the hostile host,
And crush the foe in this perilous fray."
Then the radiance faded faring on high,
And the angel with it, to the host of the holy.
The king was the blither, the captain of heroes,
And the freer from sorrow in his inmost soul
By virtue of that vision so wondrous fair.
Then Constantine, the glorious king,
Protector of princes and Giver of gifts,
War-lord of armies, bade quickly work
And shape a symbol like the Cross of Christ
As he saw that sign revealed in the heavens.
He bade at dawn, at the break of day,
Rouse the warriors to the weapon-storm,
Lift high the standard, the Holy Tree,
In the thick of the foe bear the Cross before them.
Loud o'er the legions the trumpets sang.
The raven rejoiced; the wet-winged eagle
Gazed on the struggle, the cruel strife;
The wolf, woodland comrade, lifted his wail.
Battle-terror was come. Then was crashing of shields,

Crush of heroes and hard hand-swing,
The slaughter of many, when first they met
The flying darts. Against the doomed
The stalwart fighters with strong hand
Sent storms of arrows, their battle-adders,
O'er the yellow shield on the savage foe.
Stout-hearted they stormed, fiercely attacking;
Broke through the shield-hedge; drove home the sword.
Before the legions the banner was lifted,
The war-song was sung. Helmets of gold
And spear-points flashed on the field of war.
The pagans perished; peaceless they fell.
  Then headlong fled the Hunnish folk
When the Roman war-lord waging the fight
Bade lift on high the Holy Tree.
Heroes were scattered; some war took;
Some barely survived in the bitter fight;
Some half-alive fled to a fastness,
Sheltered themselves in the stony cliffs,
Beside the Danube defended a stronghold;
And some at life's end drowned in the river-depths.
  Then the heroes exulted pursuing the heathen
Until evening came from the dawn of day;
Ash-spears flew, their battle-adders.
The host was cut down, the hated horde;
Of the Hunnish troops but few returned home.
So was it clear that the King Almighty
Awarded to Constantine in that day's work
Fortune in battle, glory and fame
And an earthly kingdom, through the Holy Cross.

Two Rune Signatures of Cynewulf

The *Juliana* Signature*

I have great need that the Saint grant help
When the dearest of all things undo their union;
When the two that were married dissolve their tie,
Their binding love, and my soul leaves body
Going its way I know not whither,
Not knowing the realm. From this I shall come
To another country according to my deeds,
And my works that are past. Sadly shall depart
C, Y, and **N.** The King will be stern,
The Lord of triumph, when stained with sin
E, W, and **U** shall await in terror
What the Judge may ordain according to past deeds,
As reward for life. **L, F** shall tremble
And wretchedly wait; shall remember the wrong,
The wounds of evil that early or late
I wrought in the world. In that hour weeping
I shall mourn with tears. Too late was the time
When first I shamed me of my deeds of sin
While body and spirit sojourned together
United on earth. I have need of mercy
That the Saint intercede with the King of kings;
My need forewarns me, and sorrow of soul.
I beseech each man of the race of men,
Who recites this lay, that with fervor and zeal
He will be mindful of me by name,
And pray Heaven's Lord to grant me help,
The God of Might on the Great Day,
The Father and Comforter in that fearful hour,
The Judge of deeds and the dear Son,

* *Juliana* 695–731.

When the Trinity sitting enthroned in glory,
One in three, shall award to men
Through the radiant world, according to their works,
To each man reward. Grant us, Great God,
Thou Joy of men, that we find Thy face
Mild with mercy on that Great Day! Amen.

The *Fates of the Apostles* Signature*

Now I pray the man who may love this lay
To beseech the holy band for help in my sorrow,
For peace and repose. I have great need
Of gentle friends, and kind, on the journey
When I seek out alone my long home,
That unknown lodging, leaving behind
This mortal body, this bit of earth,
To serve as pillage and plunder for worms.
  Here may a man of clever mind,
Who has pleasure in poems, find for himself
Who composed this poem. *Wealth* (**F**) stands at the end;
Men have it on earth, can not hold it forever;
Our (**U**) worldly *Joy* (**W**) fades and the fleeting beauty
Of flesh decays as the *Water* (**L**) flows.
Then *Brave* (**C**) and *Wretched* (**Y**) shall seek for strength
In the weary night-watches; upon them lies *Need* (**N**),
The service of the King. Now can you know
Who in these words was unknown to men.
May he remember who loves this lay
To ask for me God's comfort and aid.
For I must go forth far hence alone
Seeking a home, setting out on a journey
I know not whither out of this world.
Unknown are those dwellings, that region and realm.

* *Fates of the Apostles* 88–113.

Advent Lyrics *

[I]

. . . . to the King.
Thou art the wall-stone the workers rejected
Of old from the work. It befits Thee well
That Thou shouldest be Head of the Great Hall,
Locking together the long walls,
The flint unbroken, in firm embrace,
That ever on earth the eyes of all
May look with wonder on the Lord of glory.
  With cunning skill display Thy craft
Triumphant, Righteous, and quickly raise
Wall against wall. The work has need
That the Craftsman come, the King Himself;
That He then rebuild what now is broken,
The house under roof. He wrought the body,
The limbs, of clay; now the Lord of life
From their foes must rescue this wretched host,
The woeful from dread, as He oft has done.

[III]

  O holy Jerusalem, Vision of peace,
Fairest of royal seats, City of Christ,
Homeland of angels, in thee for ever
Rest the souls of the righteous alone
In glory exulting. No sign of sin
In that city-dwelling shall ever be seen;
But from thee all evil shall flee afar,
All trouble and toil. Thou art wondrously filled
With holy hope, as thy name is named.

* *Christ I* 1–17; 50–70; 249–74; 275–300.

Lift up thine eyes on the wide Creation,
The dome of heaven, on every hand;
Behold His coming: The King of glory
Himself approaches to seek thee out,
To abide in thee, as the blessed prophets
In their books foretold the birth of the Christ,
To thy comfort spoke, thou fairest of cities!
Now is the Babe come born to transform
The works of the Hebrews. He brings thee bliss,
Looses the bonds that lie upon men;
For He it is knows the harrowing need,
How man in his wretchedness waits for mercy.

[VIII]

Bless earth with Thine Advent, O Saviour Christ!
And the golden gates which in days gone by
Full long stood locked, High Lord of heaven,
Bid Thou swing open and seek us out,
Humbly descending Thyself to earth.
We have need of Thy mercy. The dark Death-Shadow,
The Accursed Wolf, has scattered Thy sheep
And widely dispersed them; what Thou, O Lord,
Bought with Thy blood, that doth the Wicked One
Take into bondage, and smiteth sore
Against our desire. O Saviour Lord,
In our inmost thoughts we eagerly beg:
Hasten to help us, miserable sinners,
That the Prince of torment may plunge to hell;
And Thy handiwork mount up on high,
Creator of men, and come to righteousness,
To the beauteous realms in the land above
From which the Dark Spirit led us astray,
Beguiled and seduced us through grievous sin

So that, shorn of glory, unto all ages
We must suffer affliction, except Thou first
O Living God, Eternal Lord,
Shield of all creatures, shall will to save us
Out of the clutch of the Foe of mankind.

[IX]

Hail, O most worthy in all the world!
Thou purest Maiden that ever on earth
Through the long ages lived among men!
Rightly all mortals in blithe mood
Name thee blessed and hail thee Bride
Of the King of glory. The thanes of Christ,
In heaven the highest, carol and sing
Proclaiming thee Lady of the heavenly legions,
Of earthly orders, and the hosts of hell.
Thou only of women didst purpose of old
To bring thy maidhood unto thy Maker,
Presenting it there unspotted of sin.
Of all mankind there came no other,
No bride with linked jewels, like unto thee
With pure heart sending thy glorious gift
To its heavenly home. The Lord of triumph
Sent forth His herald from the hosts on high
To bring thee knowledge of abundant grace:
That in pure birth thou shouldst bear God's Son
In mercy to men; and thou thyself, Mary,
Remain for ever Immaculate Maid.

A Dream of the Rood

Lo! I will tell the dearest of dreams
That I dreamed in the midnight when mortal men implies not mortal
Were sunk in slumber. Me-seemed I saw
A wondrous Tree towering in air,
Most shining of crosses compassed with light.
Brightly that beacon was gilded with gold;
Jewels adorned it fair at the foot,
Five on the shoulder-beam, blazing in splendor.
Through all creation the angels of God
Beheld it shining— no cross of shame!
Holy spirits gazed on its gleaming,
Men upon earth and all this great creation.
Wondrous that Tree, that Token of triumph,
And I a transgressor soiled with my sins!
I gazed on the Rood arrayed in glory,
Shining in beauty and gilded with gold,
The Cross of the Saviour beset with gems.
But through the gold-work outgleamed a token
Of the ancient evil of sinful men
Where the Rood on its right side once sweat blood.
Saddened and rueful, smitten with terror
At the wondrous Vision, I saw the Cross
Swiftly varying vesture and hue,
Now wet and stained with the Blood outwelling,
Now fairly jeweled with gold and gems.
Then, as I lay there, long I gazed
In rue and sadness on my Saviour's Tree,
Till I heard in dream how the Cross addressed me,
Of all woods worthiest, speaking these words:
"Long years ago (well yet I remember)
They hewed me down on the edge of the holt,
Severed my trunk; strong foemen took me,

For a spectacle wrought me, a gallows for rogues.
High on their shoulders they bore me to hilltop,
Fastened me firmly, an army of foes!
"Then I saw the King of all mankind
In brave mood hasting to mount upon me.
Refuse I dared not, nor bow nor break,
Though I felt earth's confines shudder in fear;
All foes I might fell, yet still I stood fast.
"Then the young Warrior, God, the All-Wielder,
Put off His raiment, steadfast and strong;
With lordly mood in the sight of many
He mounted the Cross to redeem mankind.
When the Hero clasped me I trembled in terror,
But I dared not bow me nor bend to earth;
I must needs stand fast. Upraised as the Rood
I held the High King, the Lord of heaven.
I dared not bow! With black nails driven
Those sinners pierced me; the prints are clear,
The open wounds. I dared injure none.
They mocked us both. I was wet with blood
From the Hero's side when He sent forth His spirit.
"Many a bale I bore on that hillside
Seeing the Lord in agony outstretched.
Black darkness covered with clouds God's body,
That radiant splendor. Shadow went forth
Wan under heaven; all creation wept
Bewailing the King's death. Christ was on the Cross.
"Then many came quickly, faring from far,
Hurrying to the Prince. I beheld it all.
Sorely smitten with sorrow in meekness I bowed
To the hands of men. From His heavy and bitter pain
They lifted Almighty God. Those warriors left me
Standing bespattered with blood; I was wounded with spears.
Limb-weary they laid Him down; they stood at His head,
Looked on the Lord of heaven as He lay there at rest

From His bitter ordeal all forspent. In sight of His slayers
They made Him a sepulcher carved from the shining ston
Therein laid the Lord of triumph. At evening tide
Sadly they sang their dirges and wearily turned away
From their lordly Prince; there He lay all still and alone.

"There at our station a long time we stood
Sorrowfully weeping after the wailing of men
Had died away. The corpse grew cold,
The fair life-dwelling. Down to earth
Men hacked and felled us, a grievous fate!
They dug a pit and buried us deep.
But there God's friends and followers found me
And graced me with treasure of silver and gold.

"Now may you learn, O man beloved,
The bitter sorrows that I have borne,
The work of caitiffs. But the time is come
That men upon earth and through all creation
Show me honor and bow to this sign.
On me a while God's Son once suffered;
Now I tower under heaven in glory attired
With healing for all that hold me in awe.
Of old I was once the most woeful of tortures,
Most hateful to all men, till I opened for them
The true Way of life. Lo! the Lord of glory,
The Warden of heaven, above all wood
Has glorified me as Almighty God
Has honored His Mother, even Mary herself,
Over all womankind in the eyes of men.

"Now I give you bidding, O man beloved,
Reveal this Vision to the sons of men,
And clearly tell of the Tree of glory
Whereon God suffered for man's many sins
And the evil that Adam once wrought of old.

"Death He suffered, but our Saviour rose
By virtue of His great might as a help to men.

He ascended to heaven. But hither again
He shall come unto earth to seek mankind,
The Lord Himself on the Day of Doom,
Almighty God with His angel hosts.
And then will He judge, Who has power of judgment,
To each man according as here on earth
In this fleeting life he shall win reward.
"Nor there may any be free from fear
Hearing the words which the Wielder shall utter.
He shall ask before many: Where is the man
Who would taste bitter death as He did on the Tree?
And all shall be fearful and few shall know
What to say unto Christ. But none at His Coming
Shall need to fear if he bears in his breast
This best of symbols; and every soul
From the ways of earth through the Cross shall come
To heavenly glory, who would dwell with God."
Then with ardent spirit and earnest zeal,
Companionless, lonely, I prayed to the Cross.
My soul was fain of death. I had endured
Many an hour of longing. It is my life's hope
That I may turn to this Token of triumph,
I above all men, and revere it well.
This is my heart's desire, and all my hope
Waits on the Cross. In this world now
I have few powerful friends; they have fared hence
Away from these earthly gauds seeking the King of glory,
Dwelling now with the High Father in heaven above,
Abiding in rapture. Each day I dream
Of the hour when the Cross of my Lord, whereof here on earth
I once had vision, from this fleeting life may fetch me
And bring me where is great gladness and heavenly bliss,
Where the people of God are planted and stablished for ever
In joy everlasting. There may it lodge me
Where I may abide in glory knowing bliss with the saints.

May the Lord be gracious who on earth of old
Once suffered on the Cross for the sins of men.
He redeemed us, endowed us with life and a heavenly home
Therein was hope renewed with blessing and bliss
For those who endured the burning. In that great deed
God's Son was triumphant, possessing power and strength!
Almighty, Sole-Ruling He came to the kingdom of God
Bringing a host of souls to angelic bliss,
To join the saints who abode in the splendor of glory,
When the Lord, Almighty God, came again to His throne.

The Last Judgment *

Suddenly in the midnight on mortal men
The Great Day of the Lord God shall come with might,
Filling with fear the fair Creation,
Like a wily thief who walks in darkness,
A robber bold in the black night
Who suddenly assails men fast in slumber,
Lying in wait for the unwary and the unprepared.
So on Mount Sion a mighty host
Shall gather together faithful to God,
Bright and blithe; they shall know bliss.
From the four regions of earth's realm,
From the uttermost corners of earth's kingdom,
All-shining angels in unison sounding
Shall blow their trumpets in a great blast.
The earth shall tremble, the mold under men.
Loud shall resound the strains of the trumpets
Swelling clear to the course of the stars.
They shall peal and sing from south and north,
From east and west over all creation.
They shall wake from death the sons of warriors,
All mankind, from the ancient earth
To the terror of Judgment, telling them rise,
Start up straightway from their deep sleep. . . .
Suddenly on Mount Sion from the south and east
Shall come from the Creator light like the sun
Shining more bright than men may imagine,
Gleaming in splendor, when the Son of God
Through the arching heavens hither appears.
Then comes the wondrous presence of Christ,
The glory of the Great King, from the eastern skies,
Cordial and kind to His own people,
Severe to the sinful, wondrously varying:

* *Christ* 3 867–89; 899–991; 1027–38; 1061–1102; 1634–64.

Unto the blessed and the forlorn unlike!
  To all the good He is gracious of aspect,
Winsome and blithe to that holy band,
Joyous and loving, a gentle Friend.
'Tis a pleasant sight and sweet to His dear ones,
That shining beauty gentle in joy,
The Coming of the Saviour, the King of might,
To all who earlier here on earth
Pleased Him well by their words and works.
  But to transgressors, to guilty souls
Who come before Him destroyed by sin
He shall be fearful and frightful to see.
This may serve as a warning of woe for sinners
That a man of wisdom need feel no dismay,
No whit of dread in the Day of Doom.
In the face of that terror he shall not fear
When he sees the Shaper of all Creation
Moving to Judgment with wondrous might,
And round Him circling on every side
The angel multitude in shining muster,
Hosts of the holy throng upon throng.
  There is din through the deep Creation. Before God
The greatest of raging fires flames over earth.
The hot blaze surges, the heavens shall fall;
The steadfast light of the stars shall fail.
The sun shall be blackened to the hue of blood
Which shone so brightly for the sons of men
Over the ancient earth. The moon herself
That by night illumined mankind with her light
Shall sink from her station; so also the stars
Swept by the whirlwind through the storm-beat air
Shall vanish from heaven.
                With His angel host
The Lord of kings shall come to the Judgment,
The glorious Ruler; His gladsome thanes,
The hosts of the holy, shall attend their Lord
When the Prince of men amid pangs of terror

Himself shall seek out the peoples of earth.
Then loud shall be heard through the wide world
The sound of heaven's trumpet; on seven sides
The winds shall rage raving in uproar;
They shall wake and wither the world with storm;
They shall fill with fear the creatures of earth.
Then shall be heard the heaviest of crashes,
Mighty and deafening, a measureless blast,
The greatest of tumults, terrible to men.
There the doomed hordes and hosts of mankind
Shall turn away to the towering flames
Where consuming fire shall seize them alive,
Some above, some below, filled full of flame.
Then shall be clear how the kin of Adam
Full of sorrow weep in distress,
Nor for little cause, those hapless legions,
But for the greatest of all griefs
When the dark surge of fire, the dusky flame,
Seizes all three: the seas with their fish,
The earth with her hills, and the high heavens
Bright with stars. The destroying fire
In fiercest fury shall burn all three
Grimly together. And all the earth
Shall moan in misery in that awful hour.
So the greedy spirit, the despoiling brands,
Shall search through earth and her high-built halls;
The wide-known blaze burning and greedy
Shall fill the world with a terror of flame.
Broken city-walls shall crumble and crash;
Mountains shall melt, and the high cliffs
Which in olden days shielded the earth
Stout and steadfast against the floods,
Barriers against the waters, the breaking waves.
In that dread hour the death-fire shall clutch
Every creature of bird and beast.
The fire-dark flame shall fare through earth
A raging warrior. As waters of old,

The rushing floods, flowed over earth,
In that hour shall burn in a bath of fire
All the fishes cut off from the sea;
All beasts of the deep shall wretchedly die.
Water shall burn like wax. And then shall be
More of marvels than man can imagine:
How the thunder and storm and the wild wind
Shatter the wide Creation. . . .
Straightway all of Adam's kin
Shall be clothed with flesh, shall come to an end
Of their rest in earth; each of mankind
Shall rise up living, put on body and limbs,
Made young again at the Coming of Christ.
Each shall have on him of evil or good
All his soul garnered in years gone by,
Shall have both together, body and soul.
Then the manner of his works, and the memory of his words,
The hidden musing of his inmost heart,
Shall come to light before heaven's King. . . .
Then the trumpet's strain and the shining standard,
The fiery heat and the heavenly host,
The throng of angels and the throes of fear,
The Day of terror and the towering Cross
Upraised as a sign of the Ruler's might,
Shall summon mankind before the King,
Every soul that early or late
Was fashioned in flesh with limbs and body.
Then the greatest of legions, living and young,
Shall go before the face of the Lord God.
By need and by desire known by their names
They shall bring to God's Son the hoard of the breast,
The jewels of life. The Father will learn
How safely his sons have guarded their souls
In the former land where they lived on earth.
Those shall be bold who bring unto God
A shining beauty. Their strength and joy
Shall be greatly abundant to bless their souls,

To reward their works. Well is it with them
Who find favor with God in that grim hour!
There sin-stained men in anguish of spirit
Shall see as their fate the most fearful of woes:
It shall bring them no grace that the brightest of beacons,
The Rood of our Saviour, red with His blood,
Over-run with bright gore, upreared before men,
With radiant light shall illumine the wide Creation.
No shadows shall lurk where the light of the Cross
Streams on all nations. Yet shall it stand
As a woe and a menace for evil men,
Sinners who gave no thanks to God
That for man's transgressions He grievously hung
On the holy Tree, where with love our Lord
Bought life for men with His ransoming body
(Which had wrought no evil nor any wrong)
Whereby He redeemed us. For that He ordains
A stern requital when the red-stained Rood
Shall shine in splendor in the place of the sun. . . .
Then chosen souls shall bring before Christ
Their bright treasures; their bliss shall live
In the Day of Doom. They shall joy with God
In the sweet life assigned to the saints
In the heavenly kingdom. That is the home
That knows no ending, but there for ever
The pure have delight in praising the Lord,
Dear Warden of life, in light encompassed,
Swathed in peace, shielded from sorrow,
Honored with grace, endeared unto God.
Always for ever the angel band
Bright with glory shall blissfully joy
In the worship of God. The Warden of all
Shall have and shall hold the hosts of the holy.
There is song of angels and bliss of the saints,
The Saviour's dear presence shining more bright
On all His beloved than light of the sun.
There is love of dear ones; life without death;

Exultant multitudes; youth without age;
The splendor of heaven's hosts; health without pain;
For the souls of the righteous rest without toil.
There is glory of the saints; day without darkness
Bright with blessing; bliss without sorrow;
Accord among friends without envy for ever
For the happy in heaven; love without hate
In that holy throng. No hunger there nor thirst,
Nor sleep nor sickness nor burning sun,
Nor cold nor care. But the band of the blessed,
Most shining of legions, shall delight for ever
In the grace of the King and glory with God.

IX

HISTORIC BATTLE POEMS

HISTORIC BATTLE POEMS

An entry in the *Anglo-Saxon Chronicle* for the year 793 records the first of the Danish raids on the Northumbrian coast. By 866 the raiding expeditions had been followed by permanent encampment on English soil. In 870 the *Chronicle* records the havoc wrought at Medhamsted to which the Danes came, "burning and breaking and slaying Abbot and monks and all that they found." It is fitting that the defense of England in the ninth and tenth centuries should be symbolized in Old English poetry by the memorable poems of *Brunanburh* and *Maldon.*

The Battle of Brunanburh is one of a group of short poems included among the entries in the *Chronicle,* in this instance for the year 937. In it patriotic spirit and a note of national destiny receive dramatic expression. The poem has sometimes been misunderstood because of its failure to name individual heroes, or recount individual exploits. But *Brunanburh* was never intended to be a detailed description of the battle. It is rather a chant of triumph celebrating one of those decisive military successes that mark the development of national unity and national strength. The precise location of the battle has not been identified with certainty, but Bosworth placed the battle "about five miles southwest of Durham."

The Battle of Maldon was preserved in a manuscript of the Cotton collection. It celebrates a bitter but glorious defeat, whereas *Brunanburh* celebrates a great victory. According to the account of the battle in an entry in the *Chronicle* for 991, the Viking forces sailed up the Blackwater (Panta) and established a temporary base near Maldon. Laborde (*English Historical Review* xi, 161) believes that this base was on Northey Island, from which the invaders crossed to the mainland at the beginning of the battle. From the western end of the island the river bed ridges up into a ford to the mainland, which is partly exposed at low tide, but completely covered at high water. This is presumably the "bricg" or "ford" of lines 74, 78, 81, and 88 of the poem.

The death of Byrhtnoth, leader of the English forces, is followed in the poem by the most extended and realistic depiction of *comitatus* loyalty in Old English verse. The poet calls the bloody roll of honor. Warrior after warrior is named, and his heroism recounted. Fighting shoulder to shoulder with the young and strong, the aged Byrhtwold glorified his last battle with a clarion call to fortitude and death, whose echo lives while friendship and loyalty are dear and men defend the things they love. His words set the mood of all heroic striving in which deep-seated devotion to a moral imperative breeds a contempt for the odds of battle.

The Battle of Brunanburh

Æthelstan King, lord of eorls,
Ring-bestower, and also his brother,
Edmund Ætheling, won with the sword-edge
Lifelong glory in battle at Brunanburh.
They cut their way through the wall of shields,
Hacked the bucklers with hammered blades.
Such was the way of the sons of Eadweard,
Ever in battle with every foe
Defending their land, their hoard and their homes.
Foemen fell, the Scottish squadrons,
Ship-warriors also doomed to death.
The field was wet with the blood of battle
From the hour of dawn when the shining sun,
God's radiant candle, rose over earth
Till the noble creation sank to its setting.
Wounded with spears lay many a warrior,
Many a northern man shot over shield;
Scotsmen likewise sated with war.
All day long the West Saxon army
Followed the track of the hated foe,
Smote them down with sharp-edged swords.
The Mercians refused fierce hand-play to none
Of those who with Olaf over the sea
Sought this land in their broad-beamed ships,
Fated in war. Five young kings
Fell on the battlefield slain with swords;
Also seven of the eorls of Olaf
And a countless number of shipmen and Scots.
The prince of the Northmen was put to flight,
With a little band beaten back to his boat.
The ship was launched; the prince set sail
On the fallow surges and saved his skin.
Likewise also the aged Constantine

Fled in haste to his home in the north;
The white-haired warrior had no need to boast
Of that crossing of swords. He was shorn of kin,
Bereft of friends struck down in the fight
On the field of carnage. There amid corpses
He left his son, a stripling in battle
Broken with wounds. The gray-haired warrior,
The crafty old captain, had no cause to boast
Of the clash of swords, nor had Olaf any!
The few that were left had no need to laugh,
Or boast they were better in works of war,
On the field of battle, mid clash of banners,
Crashing of fighters and casting of spears,
In the storm of weapons, the carnage of war,
When they fought their fight with the sons of Eadweard.
The Northmen embarked in their well-nailed boats,
Bloody survivors of battle-spears,
Over Dinges Water returning to Dublin,
Back to Ireland, broken in mood.
Likewise also the brothers together,
King and prince returned to their people,
To the West Saxon country, proud of the war.
They left behind them to feast on the fallen
The dark raven, the dusky-coated
With horny beak, and the ash-feathered eagle
With white tail, and the war-hawk greedy
Gorging on carrion, and that gray beast,
The wolf in the wood. Nor of greater slaughter
In all this island was tale ever told
By scholar or book, or more folk felled
Slain by the sword, since hither from East
The Angles and Saxons sailed over sea,
Over broad billows seeking out Britain,
Great-hearted war-smiths eager for honor
Who harried the Welshmen and held the land.

The Battle of Maldon

. . . . was broken.
He bade a warrior abandon his horse
And hurry forward to join the fighters,
Take thought to his hands and a stout heart.
Then Offa's kinsmen knew that the eorl
Would never suffer weakness or fear;
And he let from hand his beloved hawk
Fly to the forest, and made haste to the front;
By which one could know the lad would never
Weaken in war when he seized a sword.
  Eadric also stood by his lord,
His prince, in the battle; forward he bore
His spear to the fight; he had firm resolve
While he could hold in hard hand-grip
Broad sword and buckler; he made good his boast
That he would battle beside his lord.
  Byrhtnoth began to hearten his fighters;
He rode and gave counsel, instructing the men
How they should stand and defend the spot.
He bade that they hold their bucklers aright
Firm in their hands, and be not afraid.
When he had fairly mustered the folk
He lighted down where it liked him well,
Where he knew his retainers were truest and best.
  Then stood on the strand and boldly shouted
The Viking herald, boastfully hurled
To the eorl on the shore the shipmen's message:
"These dauntless seamen have sent me to you,
Bade me say you must quickly send
Riches for ransom; better for you
That you buy off with tribute a battle of spears
Than that we should wage hard war against you.
Nor need we waste strength if you will consent;

But we for the gold will confirm a peace.
If you will agree, who are greatest here,
To ransom your people and promise to pay
On their own terms unto the shipmen
Gold for goodwill, and have peace at our hands,
We with the treasure will take to our ships,
Put to sea, and observe the peace."
  Byrhtnoth addressed him; brandished his shield;
Shook pliant ash-spear; speaking with words
Enraged and resolute, gave him answer:
"Hear you, sea-rover, what my people say?
The tribute they'll send you is tribute of spears,
Ancient sword-edge and poisoned point,
Weapons availing you little in war!
Pirate messenger, publish this answer,
Proclaim to your people tidings more grim:
Here stands no ignoble eorl with his army
Guarding my lord Æthelred's country and coast,
His land and his folk. The heathen shall fall
In the clash of battle. Too shameful it seems
That you with our tribute should take to your ships
Unfought, when thus far you've invaded our land.
You shall not so easily take our treasure,
But sword-edge and spear-point first shall decide,
The grim play of battle, ere tribute is granted."
  Then he bade bear buckler, warriors advance
And form their ranks on the river's edge;
Not yet, for the tide, could either attack.
The flood-tide was flowing after the ebb,
And the currents locked. Too long it seemed
Till men to battle might bear their spears.
Near Panta River in proud array
Stood the East Saxon host and the Viking horde;
Nor could either army do harm to the other
Except who through arrow-flight found his death.
  Then the flood-tide ebbed; the raiders stood ready,
The pirate army eager for war.

The lord commanded a war-hardened man
To defend the ford, Wulfstan his name,
Brave among kinsmen, Ceola's son.
He wounded with weapon the foremost man
Who first there fiercely set foot on the ford.
At Wulfstan's shoulder stood fearless fighters,
Ælfere and Maccus, a mighty pair.
Never would such take flight at the ford!
But they bravely defended against the foe
What time they were able to wield their weapons.
  When the pirates perceived and clearly saw
That they had been met by bitter bridge-wardens,
The Viking shipmen began to dissemble,
Asked for permission to make approach,
To fare over ford and take their troops.
It was then the eorl disdainfully granted
Too much ground to the hostile host.
Across cold water Byrhthelm's son
Shouted reply, and the shipmen hearkened:
"Now way is made open, come quickly to us,
Warriors to the onset; God only knows
Who shall hold sway on the field of slaughter."
  The war-wolves advanced, heeded not water,
West across Panta; the Viking host
Over shining water carried their shields.
Among his warriors Byrhtnoth stood bold
Against the grim foe; bade form with shields
The war-hedge for battle, hold firm the folk
Against the foemen. Then fighting was near,
Honor in battle. The hour was come
Doomed men must fall. A din arose.
Raven and eagle were eager for carnage;
There was uproar on earth. Men let from their hands
File-hard darts and sharp spears fly.
Bows were busy, shield stopped point,
Bitter was the battle-rush. Warriors fell
In both the armies. Young men lay dead.

Wulfmær was wounded; Byrhtnoth's kin,
His sister's son, was savagely butchered
Choosing the slaughter-bed, slain with the sword.
Then to the seamen requital was made.
I have heard that Eadweard slew one with sword,
Withheld not the blow; the fated fighter
Fell at his feet. And for that the prince
Thanked his retainer when later was time.
So resisted the stout of heart,
Young men in battle; boldly strove
Who first with spear, warrior with weapon,
Could visit death on life that was doomed.
There was slaughter on earth; steadfast they stood,
And Byrhtnoth heartened them, bidding each man
Take thought to the war who would win from the Danes.
The battle-hard brandished his weapon for war,
His shield for defense, and stormed at the foe;
Even so bold went eorl against churl.
Both purposed evil, each for the other.
Then the shipman cast a southern spear
And the lord of warriors suffered a wound.
He thrust with his shield so the shaft was shattered,
The lance was broken, the parts fell back.
The prince was angered; he stung with his spear
The arrogant Viking who gave him the wound.
He fought with skill driving his dart
Through the pirate's throat; he thrust with hand
So he touched the life of the savage foe.
Then most quickly he cast another
And the byrny burst. He was wounded in breast
Through his woven mail, and the poisoned point
Bit at his heart. The eorl was the blither;
The proud man laughed, gave thanks to God
For that day's work which the Lord had granted.
But one of the shipmen hurled from his hand
A flying spear; and the speeding dart
Pierced through Æthelred's princely thane.

A stripling lad stood at his shoulder,
A boy in the battle, who bravely drew
The bloody spear from the warrior's side,
Wulmær the youthful, Wulfstan's son.
Back he hurled the battle-hard dart;
The point pierced in and he sank to earth
Whose hand had given the grievous hurt.
Then a pirate warrior went to the eorl;
Soon would he seize his jewels and gems,
His armor of rings, and his well-wrought sword.
But Byrhtnoth snatched his sword from the sheath,
Broad and brown-edged, and struck at his byrny.
Too speedily one of the shipmen hindered,
Striking aside the arm of the eorl;
And the gold-hilted sword fell to the ground,
Nor might he hold longer the hard blade,
Or wield his weapon. Once more he spoke;
The aged ruler rallied his men,
Bade them go forward and bear them well.
No more could he stand firm on his feet,
But he looked to heaven. . . .
"I give Thee thanks, O God of men,
For all the joys I have had on earth.
O Lord of mercy, I have most need
That now Thou wilt grant me good to my soul,
That my spirit may come into Thy kingdom,
O Prince of angels, departing in peace
Into Thy power. To Thee I pray
No fiend of hell may have hold upon me."
Then the heathen scoundrels hacked him down
And both the fighters who stood at his side.
Ælfnoth and Wulmær both were fallen;
They laid down their lives beside their lord.
Then fled from the battle who feared to be there:
The sons of Odda were first in flight,
Godric from battle, leaving his lord
Who had given him many a goodly steed;

He leaped on the horse that belonged to his leader,
Rode in the trappings that were not his right,
And his brothers with him both galloped off.
Godrinc and Godwig recked not of war,
But turned from the fighting, took to the wood,
Fled to the fastness, and saved their lives;
And more of men than was any way right
If they had remembered the many gifts
Their lord had given them to their good.
As Offa once said, at an earlier time
In the meeting-place when he held assembly,
That many were there making brave boasts
Who would never hold out in the hour of need.
Then was fallen the lord of the folk,
Æthelred's eorl; and his hearth-companions
All beheld that their lord lay dead.
Forward they pressed, the proud retainers,
Fiercely charged those fearless thanes.
Each of them wished one thing of two:
To avenge his leader or lose his life.
Ælfric's son spurred them to battle,
A warrior young; in words that were bold
Ælfwine spoke, undaunted of spirit:
"Take thought of the times when we talked at mead
Seated on benches making our boasts,
Warriors in hall, concerning hard battle.
Now comes the test who truly is bold!
I purpose to prove my lineage to all men:
That in Mercia I come of a mighty clan;
Ealhelm the name of my aged father,
A powerful ealdorman wealthy and wise.
None shall reproach me among that people
That I was willing to slink from the strife,
Hastening home when my lord lies dead,
Slain in the battle. Of all disasters
That to me is the greatest of griefs,
For he was my kinsman; he was my lord."

Then he dashed forward, took thought of the feud;
One of the shipmen he stabbed with spear
Among the folk, and he fell to earth
Slain with weapon. He encouraged his comrades,
Friends and companions to press to the front.
Offa spoke and brandished his ash-spear:
"Now hast thou, Ælfwine, heartened us all
In the hour of need. Now our lord lies dead,
Our eorl on earth, there is need that we all,
Each of us here embolden the others,
Warriors to combat, while hand may bear
Good sword and spear, and hold hard blade.
This sneaking Godric, Odda's son,
Has betrayed us all; for when he rode off
Sitting on horse, on our lord's proud steed,
Many men weened that it was our lord.
On the field of fate now the folk is divided,
The shield-hedge is shattered; cursed be his deed
That he caused so many to flee from the fight."
Leofsunu spoke, lifted his buckler,
His board for protection, making his boast:
"I promise you here I will never turn hence
Or flee one foot, but I'll fight in the front,
In the bitter strife, and avenge my lord.
Steadfast warriors by the River Stour
Shall never have need of words to reproach me,
Now my lord is fallen, that lordless I fled,
Turned back from the battle and went to my home;
But weapon shall take me, sword-edge and spear."
Then in rage he rushed to the fighting
Despising to flee.
Dunnere shook spear,
The aged churl, called out to them all,
Bidding take vengeance for Byrhtnoth's fall:
"He may not weaken who thinks to avenge
His lord on this folk, nor fear for his life."
Then they rushed forward, recked not of life,

Household-retainers fierce in the fight,
Bitter spear-bearers beseeching God
They might work revenge for their friendly lord
In death and destruction upon the foe.
Then a hostage began to give them help,
Of Northumbrian race and hardy kin,
A son of Ecglaf, Æscferth his name.
He wavered not in the midst of the war-play
But forward pressed to the arrow-flight,
Now shooting on shield, now piercing a shipman,
But oft and often dealing a wound,
While he could wield his weapon in war.
In front line still stood Eadweard the long,
Skillful and eager; he spoke his boast:
That he would not flee foot-measure of ground
Nor turn from the battle where his better lay dead.
He shattered the shield-wall and fought with the Danes.
Upon the shipmen he stoutly avenged
His gracious lord ere he sank in the slaughter.
So did Ætheric, excellent comrade,
Sibyrht's brother; he boldly strove
Eager and ready; and many another
Stood their ground and shattered the shields.
Bucklers broke, and byrnies sang
A song of terror. Then Offa smote
One of the shipmen and laid him low;
But Gadd's kinsman also fell in the fight.
Quickly in battle was Offa cut down.
But he had performed what he promised his lord,
When he made his boast to his bracelet-bestower,
That both unharmed they would ride to the borough,
Back to their homes, or fall in the fight
And perish of wounds in the place of slaughter.
Thane-like he lay beside his lord.
Then was breaking of bucklers, shipmen advanced
Bold to the battle; sharp spears pierced
Life-house of doomed men. Wistan hastened,

Thurstan's son, and strove with the Danes.
Three he slew in the stress of battle
Ere Wiglin's son was slain in the war.
The strife was stern, warriors were steadfast,
Bold in battle; fighters fell
Weary with wounds. Death covered earth.
Oswold and Ealdwald all the while,
Both the brothers, marshalled their men;
Bade friend and kinsman endure in combat
And never weaken, but wield the sword.
Byrhtwold encouraged them, brandishing buckler,
Aged companion shaking ash-spear;
Stout were the words he spoke to his men:
"Heart must be braver, courage the bolder,
Mood the stouter as our strength grows less!
Here on the ground my good lord lies
Gory with wounds. Always will he regret it
Who now from this battle thinks to turn back.
I am old in years; I will never yield,
But here at the last beside my lord,
By the leader I love I think to lie."
And Godric to battle heartened them all;
Æthelgar's son hurled many a spear
At the Viking horde. First in the front
He hacked and hewed till he fell in the slaughter.
He was not the Godric who fled from the fight. . . .

INDEX

INDEX OF SELECTIONS

Andreas:
St. Andrew's Voyage to Mermedonia 28

Battle of Brunanburh 159

Battle of Finnsburg 66

Battle of Maldon 161

Beowulf's Last Battle:
The Fire-Dragon and the Treasure 77
Beowulf and Wiglaf Slay the Dragon 82
Beowulf's Death 87
The Funeral Pyre 92

Charm for a Sudden Stitch 70

Charm for Unfruitful Land 71

Christ and Satan:
Lamentations of the Fallen Angels 117

Christ 1:
Advent Lyrics 141

Christ 2:
The Voyage of Life 35

Christ 3:
The Last Judgment 149

Deor's Lament 57

Dream of the Rood 144

Elene:
Constantine's Vision of the Cross 135
Helena Embarks for Palestine 26

Exodus:
The Parting of the Red Sea 24

Fates of Men (Exeter Book) 49

Fates of the Apostles:
A Cynewulf Rune Signature 140

Genesis:
Noah's Flood 21
The Temptation and Fall of Man 120

Husband's Message 12

Juliana:
A Cynewulf Rune Signature 139

Lay of Finn (Beowulf) 63

Maxims (Cotton MS) 47

Maxims (Exeter Book) 51

Phoenix 102

Riddles 41

Ruin 8

Seafarer 19

Tale of Sigemund (Beowulf) 62

Waldere 68

Wanderer 5

Whale 99

Widsith the Minstrel 59

Wife's Lament 10

Date Due

SEP 30 '60			
~~DEC 1 '66~~			
~~DEC 15 '67~~			
~~MAY 20 '68~~			
MAY 7 '69			
APR 1 '70			
JUN 25 '90			

PRINTED IN U. S. A. CAT. NO. 23233